CONVERSATIONS WITI

Books by John L'Heureux

Picnic in Babylon: a Jesuit priest's journal, 1963-1967 (1967)

Novels

The Clang Birds (1972)
Tight White Collar (1972)
Jessica Fayer (1976)
A Woman Run Mad (1988)
An Honorable Profession (1991)
The Shrine at Altamira (1992)
The Handmaid of Desire (1996)
Having Everything (1999)
The Miracle (2002)

Collections of Short Stories

Family Affairs (1974)
Desires (1981)
The Priest's Wife : 13 ways of looking at a blackbird (1981)
Comedians (1990)

Collections of Poems

Quick as Dandelions (1964)
Rubrics for a Revolution (1967)
One Eye and a Measuring Rod (1968)
No Place for Hiding (1971)

Edited Collection

The Uncommon Touch: fiction and poetry from the Stanford Writing Workshop (1989)

CONVERSATIONS WITH JOHN L'HEUREUX

DIKRAN KARAGUEUZIAN

Introduction by
TOBIAS WOLFF

Center for the Study of Language and Information
Leland Stanford Junior University
Printed in the United States
14 13 12 11 10   1 2 3 4 5

Library of Congress Cataloging-in-Publication Data

L'Heureux, John.
Conversations with John L'Heureux / [interviewer, Dikran Karagueuzian] ; with an introduction by Tobias Wolff.
p. cm.
ISBN 978-1-57586-601-7 (cloth : alk. paper) –
ISBN 978-1-57586-600-0 (pbk. : alk. paper)
1. L'Heureux, John–Interviews. 2. Authors, American–20th century–Interviews. 3. Authors, American–21st century–Interviews. 4. English teachers–United States–Interviews. 5. Creative writing (Higher education)–United States. 6. Fiction–Authorship.
I. Karagueuzian, Dikran, 1940- II. Title.

PS3562.H4Z46 2010
813′.54–dc22
[B]   2010026512
CIP

∞ The acid-free paper used in this book meets the minimum requirements of the American National Standard for Information Sciences—Permanence of Paper for Printed Library Materials, ANSI Z39.48-1984.

CSLI was founded in 1983 by researchers from Stanford University, SRI International, and Xerox PARC to further the research and development of integrated theories of language, information, and computation. CSLI headquarters and CSLI Publications are located on the campus of Stanford University.

CSLI Publications reports new developments in the study of language, information, and computation. Please visit our web site at
http://cslipublications.stanford.edu/
for comments on this and other titles, as well as for changes and corrections by the author and publisher.

Contents

Acknowledgements

We wish to thank the following for permission to reproduce copyright material:

John Hughes, review of *Tight White Collar* in *Saturday Review*, 13 May 1972

Village Voice Media, Inc. for Susan Brady, 'From Celibacy to Commitment' in *Village Voice*, 17 June 1973

The Baltimore Sun Media Group for Diane J. Cole, 'Priests and Victims' in *Baltimore Sun*, 25 August 1974

The New York Times Company for Lee Grove, 'A spare, tidy novel' in *Boston Globe*, 27 May 1976

Los Angeles Times for Carolyn See, 'Short Stories Strung like Perfect Pearls' in *Los Angeles Times*, 28 April 1981

Los Angeles Times for Richard Eder, 'Nothing Recedes like Excess' in *Los Angeles Times*, 17 January 1988

Dow Jones & Company, Inc. for Lee Lescaze, 'God the Meddler' in *Wall Street Journal*, 13 February 1990

The Washington Post Company for Jonathan Yardley, 'Alone in the Classrom' in *Washington Post*, 13 October 1996

Los Angeles Times for Kathryn Harrison, 'Sanctified Madness' in *Los Angeles Times*, 19 April 1992

The Washington Post Company for John Derbyshire, 'Textual Politics' in *Washington Post*, 13 October 1996

Richard Wakefield for 'A Human Exploration' in *Seattle Times*, 3 October 1999

The New York Times Company for Bruce Bawer, 'Wonders Never Cease' in *New York Times*, 27 October 2002

Preface

When John L'Heureux had just completed his tenth novel, *The Handmaid of Desire,* anxious to read it, I asked to see the manuscript. Subsequent to my reading, we had a few conversations in my office and at the Faculty Club, most of them about the publishing world and the craft of fiction writing. Apart from the occasional chance encounter on campus, we did not meet for several years until my wife and I moved to the neighborhood where John and his wife Joan live.

In early 2005, I suggested to John that I interview him about the topics we had discussed in the past with a view to publishing the edited transcripts. At first he was reluctant but, with his characteristic generosity, conceded that the work might be of value to students of creative writing and to future historians of Stanford, given his four-decades of service to the University and his mentorship of countless students.

The interviews were done over a two-year period, at times in his office or mine. Because we were both busy, the transcription and the editing of the conversations took another two years to complete. To make the work an entirely Stanford affair, I asked Tobias Wolff to write the introduction, which he very graciously agreed to do. I would like to thank both John and Tobias for making this book possible.

—Dikran Karagueuzian
Stanford, October 2010

INTRODUCTION
by Tobias Wolff

In the summer of 1974, my brother, knowing my interest in short stories, gave me a collection he had recently read and thought I'd like—*Family Affairs,* by John L'Heureux. I loved it. What kind of man could write a sentence like this, describing a nun's self-destruction by car and bovine: "Mother Humiliata took the cow at sixty . . . "? My kind of man.

In one of my greatest strokes of fortune, I received a Wallace Stegner Fellowship a year later to study here with John L'Heureux. I also had the benefit of workshops with Richard Scowcroft and Albert Guerard, both distinguished writers and teachers, but it was John who affected me most profoundly: the rigor of his reading, the invention and boldness of his editing, and the humanity and wit of his personal presence. It was a truculent workshop in many ways, skirmishes flaring constantly along the borders of gender, politics, sexual identity and failed romances, but John could make us laugh pretty much at will, and did. Nor did he bestow this gift on us alone: I once happened to meet a man who'd been a student of his years earlier at a Jesuit high school back east. He told me that another priest had been needling John with snide messages left on the blackboard. When one of the students suggested that John engage this fellow in "a battle of wits," John declined on the grounds that he "would never fight an unarmed man."

To the stories and novels we submitted for his admiration, most of them transitional to say the least, John paid what Jane

Austen calls "the compliment of rational opposition." He was dead serious in his reading of our work, and absolutely honest in his response; after which, for those with ears to hear, he generously helped us imagine the possibilities for successful revision. He was such a good reader that for some time after I left the program I continued sending John my stories, as if he had nothing else to read.

This gift for severe and imaginative editing, for demanding that every sentence, every scene prove its worth, was not the result of training in academic analysis, though John had plenty of that, but from the experience of his own practice as a poet, novelist, and writer of short stories. In reading his work, one can see, *feel,* the demands he makes on himself for exactitude, essence, emotional honesty, aesthetic freshness, digging deep for the truths of our thoughts and desires and presenting his findings without flinching, even—no, especially—when they challenge our self-conceptions and certainties, and trouble the heart.

Read *The Shrine at Altamira.* You may think that the father in that novel is a monster, and what he does is truly monstrous, yet still he is human, and the pain and confusion and jealousy and blind fury that lead to his act are recognizable, and have their echoes in what we know of ourselves. John's work is sometimes dire in its portraiture but never contemptuous; witty as Donne is witty, that is, seriously witty; adventurous in language and form without ever being cute. He is a beautiful writer. When you read a novel like *An Honourable Profession* or *The Shrine at Altamira,* a short story like "The Anatomy of Bliss" or "Roman Ordinary," you can't help wishing you could sit down with the writer, ask him how he came to write such a work, how he came to write at all—what were the paths that led him to this life, what surprises did he encounter along the way, what encouragements, what impediments and distractions, disappointments and joys. What has he learned about the art he has practiced so well and for so long, and what has he learned from it? Who does he read with profit? Who does he read once and not read again? Why? What were his hopes as a young man? What were his parents like, what did they do?

Of course you can't ask those questions if you don't know the writer. Even as a friend, one feels hesitant to intrude. The moment is never right; you're with other friends, the wine is flowing, the talk leads elsewhere. And so this book, in which Dikran Karagueuzian has collected no less than seven probing, far-ranging conversations with John L'Heureux, has proved a particular pleasure and revelation. I have for many years been a devotee of *The Paris Review*'s Writers at Work interview series. I like the format, which is followed here. The usual demands of tact and privacy are suspended: The interviewer can put his subject on the spot, press him, open up vistas of personal history and perspective that the protocols of friendship don't allow; and that same arrangement allows the writer to speak of himself at length, as one cannot ordinarily do, or, in most cases (not, alas, all) would wish to do, and to develop lines of reflection and argument in a sustained, complex, nuanced form. And through all this one enjoys a subtle sense of drama, because this is after all an encounter between two purposeful minds, each more or less consciously but very certainly trying to shape the event to his own ends.

One learns from an interview some things interesting though perhaps not surprising, such as John's sense of mission as an artist—"to make a new thing, a good thing." But one encounters real surprises as well. Just one example of many: Those acquainted with him all know, and those who have read his work might easily guess, that John was once a Roman Catholic priest. I've never asked him directly about that passage of his life—again, my curiosity no license for infringing on his privacy—and he hasn't volunteered an account, and why should he? But I assumed that his sense of religious vocation must have been the result of years of contemplation, prayer, and encouragement, perhaps even pressure, from the Church itself; and that his leaving the priesthood years later must have been a dramatic and perhaps bitter estrangement over some issue of doctrine or perhaps resistance to, even censure of, his creative work.

The truth is a better story. It seems John made his way through school to Holy Cross with no particular vocation, though he liked to act and had some ambition of becoming an actor, even to the point of paying forty dollars for head shots for his portfolio, but, as he tells it: "I spent most of my time goofing off. Then in my second year I got derailed by Jesus. Who knows how or why? . . . I remember talking with one of my roommates about being an actor, and out of nowhere he said, 'Why don't you become a priest. You're smart enough. You have no moral impediments (he talked like that) and it's something positive and useful you could do with your life instead of wasting it as an actor.' I dismissed what he said as ridiculous, but at the moment he said it, I knew it was going to change my life."

From such moments, apparently ordinary, even banal, do the paths of our lives proceed. Here, as in his fiction, we see John's honesty—it is hardly an agonizing, heroic struggle that leads him to this decision, more like the modest mustard seed of the parable—and also his respect for the essential mystery that underlies our thoughts and actions. He does not here or elsewhere attempt to explain that mystery away.

And his leaving? Again, the truth is more interesting, and moving, than any spiritual melodrama we might imagine: "Being a priest was too hard for me. I didn't leave because I was disappointed in the Jesuits or in the Church or because I had doctrinal issues. I left because it was too hard to be the kind of priest I wanted to be and it was too important to do any other way."

There you have it; no grand gestures, no fist shaken in the face of the heavens. The human truth, simply expressed but in fact anything but simple, or inconsequential. One can only imagine what this self-knowledge cost, after so many years, and what it cost to act on it.

I'm glad he did. Otherwise I would never have come to know him, to be taught by him, to enjoy his and Joan's friendship these many years. Nor would he have taught and been *patron* to four decades' worth of young writers who, taken together in their maturity, would constitute a creditable national literature. I can't name any without naming them all, and to do so would be tedious for the reader, and a perilous exercise for me—if I forgot someone, as I surely would, I'd have an enemy for life, or at least for a few days. No, for life.

Through all these years, apprentices like me were privileged to gather at a table with John—a *round* table, no less—and read each other's work, and to leave not with a blueprint or manual or set of rules, but with an enhanced capacity for reimagining our stories. I was lucky to be there, to share in John's gifts of insight and experience, and I knew it then. The readers of this book are now invited to take their place at the table. If my experience holds true, they will go away full, and be restless to return.

INTERVIEW 1

Q: *Why do you write?*

JL: A question I ask myself every time I sit down to do it. Flannery O'Connor was once asked that question and she answered in her rather abrupt way, "Because I'm good at it." And of course she was, and only a great writer could get away with saying that. What I usually say is this: I write because I want to make a new thing, a good thing that will entertain and, I hope, disturb.

My father was an engineer and a carpenter. My mother was a pianist. They both painted. I can't build things at all and I can't paint particularly well. Nor can I sing or dance. And so I make little pieces of fiction. I used to write poems when I first began, then I wrote a novel, and after I wrote a novel I was finally able to write a short story. For a long time I wrote only short stories. For me writing is another way of making a new thing.

Q: *This construction that you refer to, that you want to "make" or "create" something: what is the motivation behind it?*

JL: Let me start negatively. I don't write for lots of money. If I did I would be extremely disappointed. Or for prizes, or for therapy, or to impress people with how smart I am. I write because I get pleasure and satisfaction from the process of writing rather than from publication itself. Publication provides its own kettle of snakes. The satisfaction in publishing something is invariably marred by disappointment. First of all, disappointment that the work itself is not the perfect thing it was in your mind. Then disappointment that it isn't received with the intelligence you think you put into it. Disappointment that people don't buy it and read it in great masses. Disappointment that reviewers misinterpret it completely. As an example, some anonymous person said on Amazon about *The Miracle*: "This is a terrible book about the faults L'Heureux finds with the Roman Catholic church, but it doesn't matter because he's an awful writer anyway." (Laughs) He said it better, as I recall, but that in essence was his review. Actually, I've been lucky with reviewers. All my books, even the four volumes of poetry, have been reviewed in the *New York Times*, and very favorably too, so I have no quarrel with reviewers. Nonetheless, publication is not one of the great pleasures of writing.

One of the genuine pleasures of writing comes when you sit down with no feeling of inspiration whatsoever and you put in your two or three hours of work, and something far better than you could have hoped—something really good—appears on the page. And it's suddenly thrilling. For that moment you think you're going to pass as a writer. Nobody will have found you out when they read this passage. The other passages will tell them everything they suspected about you and your ability or lack of it, but this passage is the work of a real writer. It's exciting to see something better than yourself emerge on the page. Better than you could have expected.

Q: *When did you first realize that you ought to become a writer?*

JL: I was very, very young. I had a cousin who was a painter, an artist, and he was at least ten years older than I. Maybe more. I remember the awe and respect with which my parents and his parents regarded his work. And with good reason, since he became a very fine artist. Early on in his career he got sidetracked into advertising and in his twenties he became a vice-president of J. Walter Thompson, but he remained a fine painter all the same. Anyhow it was clear to me that to make a painting was a very exciting thing. I realized soon enough, however, that I couldn't draw well and I couldn't paint worth a damn. But I did have some ability to make up things, little poems and stories that I brought to school to show Miss Connolly—the love of my life in the fourth grade—and she encouraged me to write more. Also there were no kids my age where I lived so I read all the time, and if books are your life, that has its own effect.

I remember one day when I had finished the last of The Hardy Boys series and there were no more to read and I thought, well, I wonder if I could write one. I couldn't have been more than ten years old, but I remember thinking, why not? I didn't tell anybody about this. It would've seemed vain or self-indulgent or indicated a lack of humility that was not thought well of in my family. Even to me it seemed pretentious to presume I could write a book. Still, I didn't see why I shouldn't fiddle around with it so long as I didn't tell anybody. I got serious about it by the time I was in college. In fact I published my first poem in my freshman year: it was a sonnet that appeared under another guy's name. He was in an advanced class—I was in the B section—and they had to write a sonnet. I wrote it and he handed it in and the professor asked if he could publish it in the college magazine. There was no way out for either of us. I don't remember the guy's name or the title of the poem, but my guess is that it was a metrically exact and thoroughly awful sonnet.

Q: *At this point it was not clear to you whether you'd stay with poetry or you'd be going on to fiction?*

JL: Oh, I didn't think of myself as a writer of any kind. I was just a kid fooling around. I always wanted to write fiction, but even a short story was much too ambitious for me. I didn't know basic things like plot development or point of view or the difference between scene and narrative. I just knew that whenever I started writing a story, it all fizzled by the second or third page. I was writing sketches because

I had nothing to say, really. But in poetry I found a form that was sufficiently small—a lyric poem, a 14 or 16 line poem—to admit of a single sensibility and a single tone that came together in a whole that could be moving or funny. The big revelation for me was that it was all right to be funny. And I made that discovery when I was still writing poetry.

Q: *So you had that funny, cynical side even then.*

JL: Ironic, rather than cynical.

Q: *Early on, in your childhood.*

JL: As a young man. Yeah. I was in my twenties when I began to publish poems regularly, in *The Atlantic* first and then in a lot of quarterlies.

Q: *I want to go back to the business of writing. How one develops the desire to write. William Maxwell, for example, in his* Paris Review *interview, talks about making the past right—remedying the past—or something to that effect.*

JL: Yes, that was interesting.

Q: *My take on that is this: something in the past has been missed or ignored and the author tries to compensate for that loss, tries to recreate that past and the feeling that accompanied it. Something important. For moral reasons. It's not like you missed a party . . .*

JL: Yes.

Q: *He wants to make amends with the past. What is your reaction to that?*

JL: Well, when I read the Maxwell interview I thought this must be the response of a man who comes very late to writing and who feels the need for a corrective to his life. I think most writers begin early and they aren't so much correcting a life as just trying to understand it. Or perhaps they're trying to come to terms with defects of character or personality or will that have changed their lives or could change their lives. After all, the possible is not only a source of hope; it's a source of horror as well.

Joyce Carol Oates offers a good example of what I'm trying

to get at. My wife and I were having dinner with Joyce and her husband, Ray Smith, in London—this was in 1971—and it was the first time we'd met face to face, though we had corresponded when I was a staff editor at The Atlantic. Ray and I were drinking brandy, and Joyce doesn't drink at all. All of a sudden she said, "Let me just smell that so I can see what it's like." She took my brandy and she smelled it and suddenly, as we sat there at dinner in Simple Simon's, she turned into another person. Her face convulsed and she shook her head violently and said, "Oh, if I ever touched that I could become anything, I could do anything. Something terrible could happen." And I could see that something terrible was happening right there in her imagination. It was a revelation to me of what lay beneath a very lovely, very placid surface of Joyce Oates. She's a lovely, sane, sophisticated woman. She's nothing like her fiction. She's utterly self-possessed, utterly calm. But she writes out of the possible Joyce Oates that in another world could exist and could murder people and commit arson and God knows what kind of horrible criminal acts. She has a vast number of possible selves—as did Chekhov and Dickens and Tolstoy—and she puts them in situations that develop into those myriad, wonderful novels she's produced.

Q: *I was taken by her fiction at one time. I haven't read everything she's written.*

JL: Who has? She has more than 300 listings in the Stanford library catalogue.

Q: *But what you describe seems perfectly in character for her. It's something that doesn't surprise me. I would expect a reaction like that. But, be that as it may, we were talking about the Maxwell interview.*

JL: Right. I was suggesting that most writers, and I among them, write from a perceived absence—a character deficiency or will deficiency or moral deficiency—and they draw on that to create the reality of their characters. I think this is true: in every fictional character there is some deficiency that you can probably find in the author as well. A real or imagined deficiency.

Q: *So in some sense you're agreeing with what Maxwell says and how I'm interpreting it.*

JL: No. These are two different things. Maxwell is talking about something in his past life that he's remedying in his present life. I'm talking about the phenomenon that a character becomes real only when you give him something in you that you don't like about yourself. In *The Shrine at Altamira* the kind of jealousy that drives Whitaker to set his own child on fire and, later, the cowardice that keeps him fighting for his life in jail—if it is cowardice and not just the desire to live—is something that I don't think I'm guilty of, but I see that I'm capable of it. If put in his situation, I might react as he did. Not by burning my child, but I might experience that same kind of . . . I know what jealousy is because I have felt it. It's not a beautiful feeling.

What I mean to say is that a character in my fiction never takes on a palpable reality until I give it some note of unpleasantness—that comes from me, that's part of my character, really or potentially. The reader presumes it's just another rotten thing about this character, but really it's a rotten thing about me.

Q: *So, in short, you write because . . . ?*

JL: I write for the satisfactions provided by the process itself and because there's a great pleasure in seeing a piece of work that's truly finished. Or as finished as I can make it. A book that's good in itself and good to read.

Q: *And among your books which do you think are the most finished?*

JL: One should never disown one's children, but my favorites—because they seem to me to accomplish what I set out to do—are perhaps *A Woman Run Mad, The Handmaid of Desire,* and *The Shrine at Altamira.*

Q: *That's three out of seventeen.*

JL: Three is a lot. And some of my short stories, "The Comedian," for instance, and "The Anatomy of Desire."

Q: *Let me go to another writer who once told me that the writer has a secret wish to humiliate himself.*

JL: That's plain silly. That's like saying you write to express your emotions or to practice therapy . . . as if you exorcise the desire to murder your wife by writing about a man who actually does murder his wife.

I don't know any writer who's eager for humiliation. From a funny point of view, though, you might say that every time you publish something you risk humiliation. People say, "I read your book." And the temptation is to reply, "Oh? Did you like it?" And they're not reluctant to say, "No, I didn't." Who needs that kind of humiliation? "I saw your baby. It's ugly."

Q: *Anyway, to continue with the subject of writing, you mentioned that the author assumes different personalities.*

JL: I was talking about Oates but it's true of all fiction writers from Jane Austen to William Faulkner to Z.Z. Packer.

Q: *How does that work for you, assuming different personalities?*

JL: I'm glad you asked that because I wouldn't have thought to talk about it, and it's kind of important. It's taken for granted that you assume the personality and the experience of the main character you're writing about at a given moment. But when you're writing a scene with more than one character, the temptation is to forget the point of view, the feelings, the desires, of the lesser character in that scene. What you have to do is stop and quite consciously think yourself into the inferior position. To become the minor character.

Chekhov never created a character who thinks of himself as a minor element in the story. Every character for him is the major character because each individual is the center of his own life. When I'm teaching drama I always point out that when Ibsen's characters leave the scene, they go offstage but when Chekhov's characters leave the scene, they go on to the rest of their lives. Back to the immediate point: you have to become all of the characters, especially in an intense, emotional scene. It can be exhausting, even depressing.

Q: *At one point, you mentioned, while working on a novel, you were depressed .*

JL: Yes, I had a kind of emotional collapse—certainly not a breakdown, but a deep, deep depression—when I got half way through *The Shrine at Altamira.* I had just finished the burning scene where Whitaker sets fire to his son. I went to see a psychiatrist I had seen years and years earlier. Did I tell you all this?

Q: *Not in any detail.*

JL: Okay. I went to see him and he asked, "How are you?" and I said, "I'm fine. Well, actually, I'm not fine. I'm terribly depressed." He asked what was going on in my life that might account for that and I told him about the book I was writing. When I got as far as the scene where Whitaker sets fire to his son, he said, "Well, for God's sake, no wonder you're depressed! Just stop writing the book. No one needs this book." And I realized then that the psychiatrist and I had come to a parting of the ways. He was a very smart man and I liked him a lot and I realized he was quite right. If I wanted to stop being depressed, I should walk away from the book, but by this time I was completely committed to it and I had to fight it through to the end. Finally, of course, the depression lifted.

I suppose that in a certain way it's like being an actor. You live with Macbeth long enough and you find yourself going home with murderous tendencies.

Q: *Maybe this is a frivolous question, but after a writing session—say, on something less intense than* The Shrine at Altamira—*how long does the experience stay with you? You create a character, a scene, a situation, and you get involved two or three hours. Does the world just stop?*

JL: In a way it does stop. I remember the first time I experienced that. I was still in the Jesuits, living in a Jesuit house at Harvard and rewriting a novel called *Tight White Collar,* about a priest who decides he has to leave the priesthood. In those liberated days—it was the '60s—we had drinks from 5:30 to 6:00 to wind up the teaching part of the day. Wild times. I had been working all afternoon and about 5:45 I went down to the rec room and was astonished to see the Jesuit priests who lived there and not the people I had been writing about in my fiction. For a brief moment I felt as if I was in a room full of strangers. It's never happened quite like that again, though I think you always get subsumed into the book you're writing and for a lot longer than the two or three hours when you're at work.

Q: *When do you actually put in these two or three hours?*

JL: First off, I can't write while I'm teaching. When I'm writing, I do nothing else. I write in the morning, and in the afternoon I fiddle around—that is to say, I do errands, go to the library and look up things, because there's always something you've got to research when you're writing a book, no matter how contemporary the setting. In the evening I'll watch some television or a movie with my wife, or see friends or have dinner or whatever. And then before bed, I'll spend an hour or so going over what I wrote that day, so that on the next morning it'll all be fresh in my mind. But I'm never really free of the book.

I talked to Wally Stegner about this once and he was astonished, since of course he wrote every day of the year, except on Christmas. He shook his head as if I was a puzzling and not very healthy example of what writing could do to you. And of course he produced a great body of work.

Q: *Even now, after all the years of writing, you can't write and teach at the same time? How do you get things done?*

JL: Actually, I'm semi-retired as of this year and I teach only the graduate writing workshop, three hours every Wednesday afternoon. I save Monday through Wednesday for the workshop—reading and commenting on the manuscripts—and I'm free to write during the rest of the week. Some people aren't as easily distracted as I am. Ron Hansen tells me that John Irving—they used to wrestle together—has a study and a library and God knows how many little work rooms, but he chooses to write at the kitchen table with people coming and going and carrying on. Irving must have an unusual ability to concentrate. Not me. Knowing I've got a lunch date on Wednesday will make writing on Monday and Tuesday that much more difficult. It's neurotic, I know, but that's how it is.

Q: *I'm curious about your reaction to the writer who says, "I need to have a job in order to be able to write."*

JL: I understand that and I feel the same way. I could never have survived as a writer if I had just taught writing. I need the input of real literature and dealing with it as a teacher must: interpreting it, showing why this book is unique and precious, how it got put together, and why it matters to us. Great writing provides a corrective to the merely good. I don't know how these young people—the Jones Lecturers—teach writing all day and then go home and write.

Q: *Isaac Bashevis Singer once said that he writes from 9 to 5, then gets on the subway and goes home. And the next morning he starts all over again.*

JL: I don't know how that's humanly possible, although I heard Roddy Doyle claim something similar. He writes all day long.

Q: *This was in reference to his job with a Yiddish-language newspaper. Singer's, I mean.*

JL: Well, that's different, but it's still terrible. Or heroic, depending on how you look at it.

Q: *Perhaps the stimulus he gets from interacting with other people is something he needs in order to write.*

JL: This is Isaac we're talking about? Not his brother Joseph?

Q: *Isaac.*

JL: Isaac. I taught his niece, Brett Singer, who wrote *The Petting Zoo.* She once told me that Isaac does nothing but sit in his pajamas all day long, writing. There are lots of people who write all day long and there are some—Graham Greene comes to mind—who work a little each day and produce an astonishing body of work. What matters isn't how much time you put in but the quality of work that comes out. Some writers hold down demanding jobs and still manage to write fine stuff. Editors somehow do it. E. L. Doctorow did it for years.

Q: *Maxwell too.*

JL: Maxwell is a perfect example. He's a very slow worker. He's a quiet writer, as in *So Long, See You Tomorrow.* He's not like Doctorow, who is brilliant and showy . . . in the best way, I mean. Think of *Ragtime.*

Q: *I suppose the amount of time you spend is not so important.*

JL: No, but it's interesting that every writer writes differently. Proust had to be in a cork-lined room to get anything down on paper and others can write on the subway. If I'm really on—despite what I said earlier about distractions—if I'm really on, I can write anywhere. Two of my novels I've begun on an airplane, *An Honorable Profession* and *The Handmaid of Desire.* Begun in long hand, in a notebook, as if writing weren't the most secret of acts.

Q: *I was going to ask you about that. How do you start a novel?*

JL: Ah! After I got over the notion that somehow a novel has to come out of me and my personal experience but in fact could come out of something in the newspaper or from a Jamesian dinner conversation, I began to see possibilities for stories and novels everywhere I looked. The central experience didn't have to be my own. What did have to be my own were the moral issues raised in the novel, though I hate the use of "moral" in this context; "questions of integrity" would be more exact.

An example: I was visiting Boston and watching television when there was a news flash—they had just arrested a high school teacher in front of his class on the grounds of molestation . . . "further details this evening at six." I thought, why would they arrest him in front of his class rather than in the Principal's office? What if he's innocent? How will he ever face a class again, innocent or not? And instantly it came to me, there's a novel in that: somebody is accused of a crime and has to deal with the consequences of that accusation. Suppose he's not guilty of this particular thing, but is in fact guilty of something else, perhaps a number of things. I thought about that a lot, though I did nothing with it because I was teaching at the time. About a year later I began to write the book, *An Honorable Profession.* It's about a high school teacher who is taking care of his dying mother and whose life is scattered in every direction. He's using a woman who takes care of his mother—using her for sex—and going to see his mother at the New England Medical Center right next to the red light district in Boston. Then one night, tired of being the dutiful son, he sets out looking for trouble and discovers a gay bar where he gets himself picked up for a one-night stand with some guy. Now he feels guilty for using the woman for sex and terribly guilty about the gay fling he's had, and so when he's suddenly accused of molesting a boy at school—though he hasn't done it, and couldn't imagine it—he finds himself caught in this double bind: he's absolutely innocent of the crime itself but he's haunted by internal guilt for any number of other things . . . as indeed he should be. So the novel starts with a man falsely accused but it becomes a study in the rich varieties of guilt.

When I sat down to write, I knew I had the makings of a novel here. I had been a Jesuit for seventeen years and had a life-long preoccupation with guilt: not having been the kind of Jesuit I wanted to be, not going out to people as generously as I should have, not living up to my vows of poverty, chastity, and obedience. Go ahead, heap it on, it's just guilt. Catholics of my age and persuasion know guilt intimately. So I had plenty to draw upon, and then all I had to do was project myself into the world of a high school teacher. Which was easy since I had been a high school teacher for three years, two at Fairfield Prep and one at Boston College High School. I knew what that world was like. I knew how small and mean it could be. And I knew the kids. So I only had to set the man down in a situation where he could be accused of molestation, and let the consequences unfold. Shall I go on?

Q: *Please.*

JL: Another example. *The Shrine at Altamira* came to me—whole—one day after I'd seen on television that a man had set fire to his son to get even with his wife. They flashed the boy's picture on the screen, and it was so upsetting and horrible that I actually got up and turned off the television. But over the next weeks the story kept coming back, and I never watched it, but I recall thinking that some fool is going to write a novel about this when in fact there is no human way to comprehend it. You'd have to be God or have knowledge of God's intentions. Some inexplicable, redemptive act. And as soon as I thought that, I knew the ending of the novel. It's the only novel I've ever begun knowing clearly what the ending would be, but of course I had no idea how to get there. I knew only that it would have to end in an act of complete renunciation of the self. "Greater love than this no man hath, that he lay down his life for his friend." An act as apparently senseless as submitting to crucifixion.

That's a terribly long answer. I'm sorry.

Q: *Not at all. It sounds like it's very painful for you to write scenes like that burning scene.*

JL: Yes, but—however painful—the only question is "Can I get it right?" So that the reader will feel the pain.

Q: *So there's a little sadism there.*

JL: It's not sadism; it's not sadism at all; it's a question of artistic control. I want to hold the emotion at a distance so I can capture it and make you feel how terrible it is. I don't think it's sadistic to make someone feel strongly about human cruelty; think of Oedipus, think of Medea. Sadism is what went on at Abu Ghraib and continues to go on—perhaps—at Guantanamo Bay. The Holocaust was sadistic; writing about the horrors of the Holocaust serves to remind us of human cruelty at its extreme. It's a corrective to what we are and how we act.

Great writing—I'm talking about the Greeks now, not about my own writing—great writing should upset you. It should leave you uncertain about your held truths and make you question, "How do I live my life?" or "How am I living this moment of my life?" That's not sadistic. That's something a writer can offer you: the opportunity to be really upset about yourself. (Laughs.)

Q: *On the question of feelings and writing: do you have to feel a certain way in order to write?*

JL: No, no, no. If that were the case, I'd never sit down and write at all. There'd always be some reason not to write. When I'm doing a book, I sit down every morning, Monday through Friday, and there are days when I say, "Oh, please God, strike me dead instead of letting me go on with this." In fact, most days I don't feel like writing. Some days, in the shower usually, I get an insight into what I'm actually doing instead of what I think I'm doing, and it's kind of exciting: maybe something wonderful will happen at the computer today. But you can't expect that every day. If you get it just once in a while, that will sustain you.

Q: *I think it's Robert Stone who said that sometimes he sits in front of his typewriter—or, I suppose, computer—and just stares at it or at the wall, and when he's feeling that way, sometimes he reads the Bible.*

JL: A lot of people do that, I'm told. Read something that will jump start them. I used to read *In the Heart of the Heart of the County* by William Gass. I've still never read the whole thing, though I've read the first few pages more than twenty times.

Q: *I suppose there are lots of tricks writers use to keep working even when they don't feel like it.*

JL: Flannery O'Connor once said that she kept a pail of water under her desk and sat with her feet in it. That way it was more trouble to get up and do something else than to just sit there and write.

Q: *That reminds me of a writer I know who says there are times when he can't write at all and who nevertheless forces himself to sit there instead of getting up and going to the beach or doing something else. He just sits there.*

JL: That's what I do, mostly.

Q: *Is that how we should end this interview, with you just sitting there?*

JL: Just sitting there working, I would hope.

INTERVIEW 2

Q: *Let's talk about writing novels versus writing short stories. Frank O'Connor once said that he finds writing a novel a lot more difficult than writing short stories. Do you feel the same?*

JL: Well, he was a great short story writer, no question.

Q: *Which form do you find easier? Or less difficult.*

JL: Writing anything is difficult . . . if you want to do it well. The nice thing about a short story is that it's finite. It's usually about 15 to 30 pages long, right? You can walk around with it, as you can with a lyric poem, and keep it in your head. You can't do that with a novel. You can only hold parts of a novel at any one time.

Q: *You once told me that for your graduate workshop you make an outline of the writer's story; you break it down into parts so that you can talk about them separately and together.*

JL: Right. It's a useful way to begin talking about a story, particularly one that's long and complicated: you ask what the story is trying to do, how it's trying to do it, and whether this is the best way to go about it. You want to determine if the author's choices are the best choices. If you look at the story in sections—without yet passing any judgment—you can see what you've got on the paper and how the parts build to a whole. In workshop next Wednesday we're dealing with a long story that I've broken down into eight sections because the writer has eight scenes and, when you examine them, it's clear that some of those scenes aren't pulling their weight and would be better as narrative.

Q: *How do you decide what should be narrative and what should be scene?*

JL: Well—forgive me, Henry James—not everything needs to be dramatized. Less important moments can be narrated; pivotal moments should usually be rendered as scene. They're equally important fictional strategies but they serve very different functions. When you move from narrative to scene, you move from history to drama. You move from telling the reader what happened to letting him participate in it. In a scene, dialogue and action are at their most potent and their most economical. Think of a play and you'll see what scene does. A scene takes a character from a moment of stasis and, because of what happens in that scene, it sets him down in a place where his life is changed . . . in a miniscule way perhaps, but changed. He can never go back to that other moment of stasis where the scene began. An effective scene moves your character one tick closer to the realization of his fate within the story. For good or ill.

Q: *It sounds like you're very preoccupied with the elements of craft.*

JL: Only when I talk about it. When I write, I work intuitively and let craft take care of itself.

Q: *Do you do this for your own work? Outline it? Break it down?*

JL: I do make an outline of my work, but only after the fact. That is, when I get about seventy pages into a novel I start keeping a record of what happens in each chapter to remind myself what I've done and where I've done it. It's a minimal outline of content and character. And I update it as I proceed.

Q: *It sounds like reworking the table of contents in a non-fiction book after you've finished it.*

JL: It is.

Q: *Except on a daily basis. Sometimes writers are secretive about the inner workings of the process of writing a novel. They don't feel comfortable telling exactly how it was done.*

JL: No.

Q: *They feel it would be disastrous for their reputation?*

JL: Yes.

Q: *A poor reflection on their intelligence, maybe?*

JL: Yes, or merely a giant bore. Writing a novel is a slightly surreal process, at least for me. For one thing, I'm convinced that if I talk about what I'm writing before I've written it, it will go away. For another, I think I draw on my insecurity for the energy to write. Part of writing—I don't think I'm alone in this—is keeping it bottled up inside. Which is why I'm always dismayed when somebody tells me about a novel he's going to write next summer—it's usually an undergrad—and he's got all the characters clear in his mind and he knows everything that's going to happen to them and it's going to be, like, awesome. And it will take two months. I try never to discourage that kind of innocence because I think people have to discover for themselves how easy or how difficult writing actually is.

There's a famous story about Saul Bellow. He was at the beach with a friend of his and the friend's son. The son, a college kid, was telling Bellow about the novel he was going to write as soon as he could find the time: and in the first chapter, this happens, and later this happens, and he went on for almost an hour. At the end, Bellow asked him, "What kind of typewriter are you going to use?" I think Bellow would agree that all the energy, the life, the surprises that are possible simply go away when you talk about what you haven't yet written.

Q: *They are already writing the novel as they're talking about it.*

JL: Yes, or at least they're dissipating the vital energy they need to write it. For me, writing is a secret activity. I never tell Joan, for instance—and she reads everything I write before it goes out—I never tell her even the names of my characters because what if she said, "Oh," and frowned. I'd think, "Well, maybe I've got it wrong. Maybe the character is badly named or maybe the character is not a character at all but just a jumble of ideas. Maybe the whole novel is a piece of crap." I'd go to pieces.

Let me amend that. Sometimes—rarely—I know something is absolutely right and then I'll tell her. When I was writing *A Woman Run Mad,* for instance, I introduced a little boy who is five years old, a lonely, bright-eyed and supremely ugly little boy. People turn away when they catch sight of him. He's always saying, "I saw you, I saw you," and of course what he saw becomes pivotal to the end of the book. In any case I fell in love with his physical ugliness and his charm. As soon as I got his name—Leopold—I knew it was perfect, so I told Joan and no damage was done. But in general the name is part of the person, and the person remains my secret until I'm ready to risk sending him out to the real world.

Q: *So when you've "finished" the novel, it is still some time before you're ready to send the manuscript to your agent? At what point do you show it to Joan?*

JL: Well, I show it to Joan only when there are no more places that I know have to be rewritten. There are, there will be, places I'm uncomfortable with, however, and almost invariably those are the places Joan points out as something she's not convinced by or doesn't like or, worst of all, doesn't believe for a minute. That feeling of discomfort is something to watch for. In workshop, for instance, good writers have told me over and over that the thing people found problematic in their work was the one thing they had been uncomfortable with themselves. Your subconscious tells you, "This isn't working." The trick is to listen. And respond. Virginia Woolf writes about this all the time in her diaries.

Q: *So this kind of response is a validation of the workshop process. Still, it would seem very difficult to critique a novel in a workshop.*

JL: It is. It's risky and it's painful. But if you're really tough and if the criticism is smart and practical, you can profit by it greatly. I admire writers who can do this because they sacrifice ego—no easy thing—and they risk damage to the work itself. They're very brave, very strong. I'd be simply crushed. I never had a writing workshop, you know, I never had anybody to instruct me. Whatever I know I learned by trial and error and by imitating my betters. It's a wasteful way to learn, but as a result what it took me 20 years to learn, I can pass on to you in a single year. Anybody can do that if they know their craft and are willing to share what they know. It's not always easy or fun.

But back to your original question of putting up a novel for criticism: I'd never encourage anybody to show something they feel isn't absolutely ready.

Q: *Even if it's a segment?*

JL: Let me correct myself. You're at the start of a novel. You've written the first 50 pages and you're in a quandary because you don't know if they're any good and you don't know if they're worth keeping and you need some kind of outside validation. So you put up those first 50 pages in workshop. Not infrequently, I'm happy to say, those 50 pages turn out to be worth keeping. Sometimes, of course, they're not, and then it's really awful for everybody. But even when those 50 pages are good, there's bound to be a problem of some kind. It might be, for instance, point of view: this story is being told from the first person and it should be third. I have a young friend—a wonderful writer, as a matter of fact—who several years ago wrote a 600 page novel in first person when everything about it cried out to be told in third. She finished the 600 pages in first person and she took it to a writing camp—Middlebury, I think—and the resident novelist there told her the book would be wonderful if she would just change the narrative voice from first to third person. My friend came back and told me what the expert said, and I thought, yes, it's the Jesuit definition of an expert: any sonofabitch from out of town. That's how it is sometimes, not easy and not fun. But 600 pages is a long way to go on a wrong point of view.

Q: *Why would a book cry out for a third person narrator rather than first?*

JL: I wasn't clear. Sorry. There are some experiences that by their nature are better narrated from a distance. A story of personal heroism, for instance, tends to get cloying—if not actually repugnant—when told by the hero. Or a descent into madness or addiction. There are some experiences we need to see from the outside. Immediately I hear you thinking, But what about Benjy in the first part of *The Sound and the Fury?* And I say, Yes, but that's Faulkner and the rest of us, alas, are not Faulkner.

Q: *In a conversation we had at another time, you reacted to first person narrative in a way that seemed to indicate the issue was pretty loaded. Who, me? Write in first person?*

JL: (Laughs.)

Q: *Are you personally opposed to using the first person?*

JL: I was probably overreacting at the time. I had never written in the first person except for one short story, "Maria Luz Buenvida," that was optioned for a movie with Angelica Huston. It was never filmed of course. It was a story set in an unspecified South American country and dealt with the Guardia in their steel-plated Toyotas and torture and the terrible phenomenon of the "disappeared." I remember thinking that there was no other way to tell the story than in the first person. And it seemed to have worked out okay.

Q: *Why is it that you can't write in the first person?*

JL: Well, I can, of course, but until now I've chosen not to. First person is very limiting since you're stuck in that one person's psychology. You don't have the freedom to go into other minds or to look at a scene from somebody else's angle of perception. Everything must be threaded through this one person's consciousness. You can't prepare a dramatic scene into which your narrator walks unprepared, for instance.

It's true that writers like Muriel Spark have used first person with great brilliance and freedom, so much so that you forget halfway through that the narrator is a character in the very story you're reading. Henry James was an expert at this. For me, the pitfalls and limitations are so obvious that I've kept away from it. There's an enormous freedom to third person omniscient or third person limited that you just don't find in first person. And I like the freedom to play God.

Q: *You've said that more than once. We must follow up on that.*

JL: I should be more forthcoming here and admit I'm well into a new novel that is, in fact, a first person narrative. It's set in fifteenth century Florence in the bottega of Donatello at the time of his creating the bronze David—about 1435—and what that did to him . . . and how and why. Since my main concern is Donatello's obsession, both artistic and sexual, it seems to me essential that the story to be told in the first person by an outside observer who loves him. This is the turning point in Donatello's creative life and—most art historians agree—in the development of Renaissance sculpture. Donatello's genius is finally incomprehensible; a lover's perspective is as close as I can get.

Q: *Well, you're full of surprises. What will the novel be called? Or is that one of those secrets you don't tell?*

JL: It's called *The Bronze Boy,* and the title refers not to the statue but to the boy who poses for it. That's all I'll say for now.

Q: *Going back to the earlier conversation about starting a novel: when you write, how difficult are you with yourself in trying to polish your sentences at first sitting?*

JL: When I first began writing, I wrote poetry, and in a poem it seemed dishonest to go on to line two until line one was as finished as I could make it. That habit has stayed with me and I remain a slow writer. I write only two pages a day, and if I can't do two pages with sentences that pass for polished, then I ought to give up. By polished, I don't mean heavy with metaphor. Or needlessly ornate. Or writing that draws attention to the writer and away from the story. Updike, a superb writer, is sometimes guilty of that. By polished I mean a single sentence that's pleasant to listen to—pleasant to say—in its relation to the rest of the paragraph. And what matters is not just the words in this sentence, but the words in this sentence as they work against the words in the rest of the sentences in the rest of the paragraph. I am more concerned about rhythms, the music of the language, than about the color of the language in itself. My prose in novels tends to be fairly flat, translucent . . . at least that's what I aim for. The character and what's happening to the character and what the character is doing is much more interesting to me than the filigree of the language in which that's expressed. Language should be subservient to the person. As it is, say, in Jane Austen or in Chekhov or in contemporaries like Alice Munro or William Trevor or Tobias Wolff. Toby writes a beautiful, clean, economical prose. It's always in service of the story he's telling.

Q: *How much work do you have left once you've done those two pages? I mean after the work is completed and you go back and look at it? Are you finished?*

JL: No matter how many times I go back, I find something that I think could sound better. And sometimes, after I've been over and over a passage, I worry that I'm changing it but not improving it. Sometimes when a piece has gone to galleys and it comes back to you in this new format—it's in hard, cold print—you can see what a critic sees. "This line needs three more words at the end to make it sound less flat." Even in the house copy of some of my books you'll find a word or two crossed out and other words put in. I confess I sometimes do this to other people's books as well—simplify or clarify the writing, I mean.

Q: *So is it fair to say that that's why you insist on producing on your computer imitation typewritten pages, double-spaced, typewriter font, and so on—obviously manuscript pages—when with no extra effort you could produce a nice typographic work that looks like a book page?*

JL: I resist typing that looks like book pages. I don't like margins artificially justified because then the page seems to be done. And, really, it's always in progress.

Q: *I was very, very impressed when I saw one of your books in manuscript form—*The Handmaid of Desire*—because there was something about it that was one hundred percent John L'Heureux. There wasn't a single typo in there . . .*

JL: There was. There were more than one.

Q: *Well, I found a few, but there was no negligence anywhere.*

JL: Well, of course there was. All I remember is that feeling of disbelief when you told me there were typos. Typos? In my manuscript?

Q: *I've seen lots of other manuscripts, but this one told you about the author's care with his work. The typos were human mistakes.*

JL: Alas.

INTERRUPTION: A STUDENT VISITOR HAS COME TO SEE JOHN.

Q: *Let's start fresh. We talked about the business of managing a novel, this huge body of information—plot, subplots, characters, setting, and so on—as opposed, say, to a short story which you can carry in your head. You have a vast territory and you have a destination. Is there something that can help you get to the end?*

JL: Yes, there is. I've never had much success explaining it, but I'll try again. Somebody in workshop is writing a novel and she's not at all sure where she's going and there's nothing to prevent her from shooting off to the left and keep going and going until she finds herself lost in a maze of pages far from her main story. So I always ask, is there some point at the end toward which you can move . . . not directly, because the whole point of a novel is that it's a complicated journey with many bypaths . . . but some emotional or psychological moment that will effect a kind of resolution of whatever problems you've dealt with? I don't mean resolution the way we customarily use it. In fact it might even be a perfect moment of irresolution, as at the end of Chekhov's "Lady with a Pet Dog." It has to be a moment that acknowledges the main issues you've raised in your book. You want to move toward that moment, no matter how far afield you go along the way.

Let me try again. As you make your way through a novel, you necessarily move away from the main story line and seem to go off on a tangent. You must do this—it's a novel, after all, it's a whole world you're creating—but you must also remember that whatever goes out from the through-line of the story has to be folded back into it. The more tangents there are, the richer the story will be in theme and sub-theme, in plot and sub-plot, so long as everything that departs from the main story line is folded back into it, logically and causally. Subsidiary events have to complement and complicate the main story. And what guides you along the way is the dim awareness of that thing—that moment—at the end when some new kind of stasis is achieved.

Example: in *A Woman Run Mad* I knew that the wife was eventually going to castrate and kill the husband. That was a given. That had to happen. But it would have to happen in such a way that the other people in the story would be affected by this as well, and not only affected but their lives would be radically altered. I didn't know how I was going to get there, but I knew that the castration and killing must involve everybody, and it was that which pulled me on to the final chapter.

Another example: in *An Honorable Profession* I knew there had to be vindication of some kind for the high school teacher. But first he had to be exposed to the ultimate humiliation that would take place at graduation, a big set piece, a kind of Scarlet Letter indictment. After this he could be reconciled with the Irish woman who took care of his mother. It was always my intention that she—the abused and misused Margaret—would forgive him and take him back . . . because of her strength, not out of any need. That reconciliation was what drove all the minor stories in the book, and there are a lot of them. It's a terribly long book.

A cautionary note: in *The Miracle*—a book that took years and years to write because I did three complete versions of it—I was determined, foolishly, that at the end the young priest would go off and get married while the old priest with ALS would still be alive and suffering, suspended between life and death. I just couldn't get it right: not the tone, not the passion, not even the story. It was only when I realized that the old priest—Fr. Moriarty—has got to die that I also realized he must in some way be responsible for the young priest's leaving and getting married. But it took me three full revisions to realize what now seems so obvious. Once I gave up the idea of Fr. Moriarty living on in misery, I was able to kill him off and give him as his last words, "Leave, for Christ's sake. Get out," which pulled the two priests together in a significant way. When people hear that in earlier versions Fr. Moriarty was still alive at the end, they're appalled that I could have been so stupid. But I was that stupid because I was holding on to the wrong ending.

So it helps to have that vague, undefined moment toward which the whole book moves, but sometimes—alas—it can be the wrong moment.

Q: *And you've seen this happen to other writers?*

JL: I've had people flounder for six or seven years with a novel that they just kept writing, and it kept going, but not going anywhere in particular. A novel, finally, is a story, it's an artifice, it's a made up thing that's got to have a shape, and shape necessarily involves an end. Muriel Spark refers to a novel as "a pack of lies," a notion I particularly like.

Q: *Can we talk more about structure?*

JL: If you can stand it.

Q: *You work in a linear way, so you must be aware instinctively of the architecture of a book.*

JL: Instinctively is a bit strong. Eventually, before I can get on with it, I have to know the physical shape of the novel I'm writing. That sounds peculiar, I know. I had a lot of trouble at the beginning of *The Shrine at Altamira* because I thought it was a book in three parts that would explore the family dynamics of Maria and Russell, and it was only when I realized, no, it's in four parts and explores something larger than family, that I was able to write it. The first half leads up to the moment when Russell burns the child and the second up to the moment when he and his son burn together at the end. Two equally balanced sections in each part, in balance both textually and emotionally. And then it became possible to write it. But each book I've written seems to have its own shape. It's at some point in the first 50 pages that I usually discover what the structure of a novel is to be. The exterior structure—the physical form of the novel—is determined, of course, by the nature of the story you're telling and the people who are suffering through that story.

Q: *So it would be safe to say that there is this constant interaction between the two? Between an interior and exterior structure?*

JL: Absolutely.

Q: *One influencing the other.*

JL: Right. It's much easier for some reason to write a conventional novel where you've got chapters in which an incident occurs and that incident propels you into the next chapter and perhaps a new set of characters and a third chapter in which the various people begin to come together and interact dynamically. I'm thinking of *An Honorable Profession* and its very conventional structure. It's easier to write that kind of book than, say, *The Miracle* where you've got this huge block of space in which you shift from character to character to character, all in the same time period. It's very hard to keep the reader caring about characters in section one, block number one, when you move onto block numbers 2 and 3 and introduce two or three new sets of characters. You've got to be shifty to help the reader remember and care about each one.

Q: *What do you think of writers who work with experimental structures, sometimes obsessively. I'm thinking of the French writer, Georges Perec.*

JL: Oh yes, write a whole book and never use the letter 'e'. It's quite a trick.

Q: *I wasn't referring to that. I was referring to another of his books,* Life, a User's Manual, *where the structure of the novel is shaped the way a knight moves on a chessboard.*

JL: Wow.

Q: *The apartment house, for example, where the novel takes place.*

JL: That's the kind of experimentalism that Gilbert Sorrentino was very, very big on when he taught here. I have no use for it, frankly, and no interest in it, though I think his Mulligan Stew is in places a very funny book. I recall once reading some of the lists in the book—he's very big on lists—and I remember laughing till I cried. Of course, I was half drunk at the time. But on principle I dislike anything that puts the cleverness of the writer ahead of the interests of the story. It always seems to me this kind of writer is showing he's smarter than I am . . . and I already know that. Gilbert Sorrentino used to have people write their own version of chapter 11 of *Ulysses*, and I never could grasp what the value of this was. Students enjoyed doing it, certainly, and some came away convinced they were writers. In fact I remember one woman, a journalist, who quit her job to go live in the Mendocino woods and write a whole novel based on her experience with chapter 11, so I guess it was a life changing experience for her. Sorrentino also had them take a page of their writing, cut it up into individual words, and throw them into the air like confetti. Then they had to reassemble the page as something new. It's one way to discover your words are not carved in stone—you can take any document apart and reassemble it to say something different—but isn't that generally conceded in the first place? I'm more interested in people than I am in cleverness. I don't know Perec well, but I know him well enough to say he gives me a royal pain in the ass. As does the whole OULIPO project that Sorrentino works from.

Q: *(Laughs.)*

JL: Do you like OULIPO? Or Perec? Have I given offence?

Q: *I couldn't finish the Perec novel.*

JL: Oh, really? Oh, I'm glad. I thought you might enjoy it . . . see, a lot of people enjoy that stuff as a divertissement.

There's a novel published recently by Sorrentino called *Gold Fools*. I gave away my copy, alas. I wish I had it at this moment. It's 400 and some pages and it's all questions. "Was he the cowboy that rode into town?" "Was he wearing a Stetson hat?" "Was he riding a black horse? Or was it a white horse?" "Did he rein in at the O. K. Corral?" "Did he go in and have a drink?" Four hundred pages of nothing but questions. Can you read this book? Can you stand it one more minute? I can't. I couldn't.

Q: *Well, I guess the question at this point becomes how can you sell the book?*

JL: Well, I don't know. The publisher must have thought there must be a market for it. And what do I know? Maybe it's an important episode in the history of experimental writing.

A lot of American experimental writing descends from James Joyce. And Joyce's *Ulysses* is a very great book that begins as a wonderful, engaging novel about a single day in the life of Leopold Bloom and his Joycean sidekick as they careen about the city. As Joyce gets his feet under him and begins to feel he's on the right track—and it's a track that nobody has trod before—the chapters get longer and longer and more and more self-indulgent. And pretentious.

(I realize this is heresy. I realize this marks me as a hopeless vulgarian unworthy of my chair at Stanford.) But it's these parts of the novel that so many experimentalists batten on. They take what he's done with the history of style, for instance, and figure that if they monkey around with style by omitting every third word in a sentence, they're taking Joyce even further. But it's really not possible to take *Ulysses* further. What happens to great revolutionary works of art like *Ulysses* is that some aspects of them get incorporated into the mainstream of English literature and the rest remains a monument in itself. So depth psychology and stream of consciousness and interior monologue have become commonplace in our literature, and we owe much of that to Joyce. But no one is going to produce another *Ulysses* by imitating the quirkier aspects of the irreplaceable original.

Q: *Since we're talking about other authors, who are your favorites? Is there someone you read more than others?*

JL: Two questions that should be easy. Since I was a Jesuit for 17 years, I've pretty much read my way—sloppily, I suppose—through the Greek and Latin classics and the required reading list of English and American lit. I have great reverence for a lot of writers I've read but don't want to read again: Dickens, Thackeray, the late James, for instance. Milton! I don't want to read another line of his poetry again, ever. On the other hand I go back to the great playwrights all the time—I've taught dramatic lit here for 30 years, as you know—the Greeks of course, and then Ibsen, Chekhov, Strindberg, and our near contemporaries: Beckett, Pinter, Miller, Williams, Albee, Stoppard, Shaffer, Mamet, whatever is on Broadway or in London.

Q: *Novelists?*

JL: Oh yes, that was the question, wasn't it. My favorite novelists are, let me see, Jane Austen, Tolstoy, George Eliot, and then a long leap forward to Graham Greene, Evelyn Waugh,

Muriel Spark, Flannery O'Connor: the Catholic mafia, I suppose. But I also like Malamud and Roth and Bellow. Mordecai Richler. Maggie Drabble. Barry Unsworth has written a lot of very good books; his *Sacred Hunger* is a truly great accomplishment. As is John Coetzee's *Disgrace*.

Q: *We touched on this earlier but I'm assuming that there are certain times when you're writing that you like to read X, and other times when you go to Y, and so forth. Are there particular authors you read when you're writing a particular kind of fiction?*

JL: I tend to shy away from reading fiction when I'm writing something serious. If I'm writing comedy/satire—*The Clang Birds*, say, or *Handmaid of Desire*—I might look at Muriel Spark or Evelyn Waugh. They're both great influences on my comic thinking and timing, and both are superb stylists, so it's dangerous to read them. You can easily pick up their writing tics. In general when I write fiction, I read biography or history. More likely biography than anything else. Literary biography in particular. Chekhov, Tolstoy, Austen, Byron, O'Neill, Henry James, Hemingway, Faulkner, stuff that keeps me interested but not distracted. I've taken lately to rereading the Russians. *Anna Karenina, War and Peace, The Brothers K, Crime and Punishment.* They're wonderful to read because, having read them before, I can stop at any point and not miss anything . . . and of course you always find something new and astonishing in these books.

I read for at least an hour before bed each night. I always have a reading book, something I don't have to teach. If it's something I'll teach, my brain goes into overdrive and I won't ever get to sleep. Most recently I've been rereading Graham Greene, just for the joy of seeing how he does it. He's a writer who can tell a story and make it matter . . . deeply. I'm reading *The Human Factor* for the third time, not one of his best books but a beautiful work to study just for the artistry of the structure. It's put together like some marvelous tapestry. All the colors, all the forms, everything blends so that as you read it you see each separate piece being woven in, and as you move along a picture—a story—begins to emerge, and finally it all comes together as a flawless construct. He's a brilliant technician. And of course he cares an awful lot about an artificial kind of Catholicism, one that's interesting to me because I was brought up in it. One that's more concerned with salvation and damnation than with a full, sexy Christian life . . . the kind of life one doesn't always associate with Catholicism. (Laughs.)

Q: *(Laughs.) Well, that's a subject we discussed once before and, if I were asked, I'd say you regard yourself as a sort of an outsider.*

JL: Yes. Greene, I understand, once described himself as a Catholic Agnostic which I think is brilliant. I learned this from an interviewer not long ago when he asked me about my Catholicism and I told him, "I'm kind of a free-floating Catholic." And he mentioned Greene's "Catholic Agnostic." That's a much more accurate description of what I feel I am because it suggests movement from a basic Catholicism in which I was brought up to this current position I can't define or explain or rightly understand myself, though I insist I'm still some kind of Catholic.

Q: *Would the Pope agree?*

JL: Luckily, time's up.

INTERVIEW 3

Q: *I'm going to ask you today about some of the social aspects of being a writer.*

JL: Dear God. What does that mean?

Q: *Friendships, associations, likes and dislikes, that sort of thing.*

JL: Ah, gossip!

Q: *At one time, apparently, you used to meet with fellow writers at Tresidder for breakfast every morning.*

JL: Yes, about fifteen years ago Joan and I began to go to Tresidder for a coffee and bagel instead of having breakfast at home. One day Ken Fields noticed we were there fairly regularly and he joined us. Ken, as you may know, is a very smart, funny, and charismatic guy and in a short while other people began to join us. Soon it wasn't just Joan and I having a bagel, it was a group of just about everybody who taught writing and lived close enough to campus. Eavan Boland, the Director of the Writing Program, joined us, and Toby Wolff, and sometimes Nora and Catherine—Ken's wife and Toby's wife—so six or seven of us were there quite regularly, and this went on for several years until Tresidder remodeled itself out of the breakfast business and into a rather gloomy and uncomfortable submarine sandwich shop.

Q: *How did this breakfast club end? Or why?*

JL: The usual reasons. Schedules changed, people went on sabbatical, but mostly it was a matter of Tresidder closing for almost a year. We still meet for breakfast, though not every day and not on campus. We go to the Peninsula Creamery or the Fountain in the Stanford Shopping Center. We met this morning as a matter of fact. We all remain very close friends.

Q: *And what do you talk about? Writing?*

JL: We don't talk about writing as such. As art or craft. Mostly we just talk, we just gossip.

Q: *Can you give me a sample of the gossip? Something safe?*

JL: We talked this morning about who was up for tenure and who was being postponed. And why. We'll often talk about how the graduate workshops are going; that is, who seems likely to be headed for success—whatever you mean by that. Who seems very solid. Who seems to have the most vivid private life. The gossip, I'm glad to say, is never hurtful, probably because none of the young people seem to have rip-roaring affairs any more. Or maybe they just don't let us know about them.

Q: *So you don't talk about writing?*

JL: We talk about books we're reading, that kind of thing. This morning we talked about Trollope and the film version of *He Knew He Was Right,* which turned out to be a remarkably feminist production. That surprised us generally. We talk about books by former students or friends or about some rotten piece of crap that's number one on the Best Seller List that makes us all jealous. And we talk about politics, of course, the war in Iraq, the Congress, Bush and Cheney and Condi Rice, until we work each other into a fit of anxiety and frustration and apoplexy, and then we change the subject. This morning we talked about Social Security and particularly about the current *New Yorker* and Seymour Hirsch's piece on Bush's future plans for exploration in the Middle East . . . exploration in the sense of undermining, invading, destroying in the name of Democracy. Look at me, I'm all in a sweat.

Q: *We'll change the subject back to friendships. I'd like to ask you what you thought about Hemingway and his advice to avoid the company of writers.*

JL: I wonder what he meant. Is this in a *Paris Review* interview or did he just say this to one of his hunting buddies?

Q: *In the* Paris Review.

JL: I don't know what he intended. He himself, of course, had lots and lots of writer friends. Acquaintances, I should say, since there was never a writer friend he didn't betray: Anderson, Stein, Fitzgerald, and on and on. He was a terrific name-dropper. He loved to talk about hanging out with James Joyce and going to bars where Joyce would start fights and, because he was nearly blind, he'd ask Hemingway to step in and finish the fight. Hemingway to the rescue. Ta-da! He'd beat the crap out of whoever Joyce wanted to fight with. Whomever.

Q: *Joyce would say, "Deal with him, Hemingway . . . "*

JL: In his Dublin accent. "Avoid the company of writers." I suppose he meant avoid talking about writing, schmoozing about what you're working on. It's dangerous to talk about work in progress . . . but we've been over that territory already at great length.

Do you remember that famous passage from the Hemingway profile that Lillian Ross published in *New Yorker?* She lets him hang himself, using his own words as a noose. It's about writing as basically competition. He started out slowly, he says, and he beat Turgenev. Then he trained hard and beat Maupassant and fought a couple draws with Stendahl. Modestly, he confesses reluctance to get in the ring with Tolstoy. It's ludicrous to regard writing as a prizefight. You write to be as good as you can be, and if that means you write as well as Turgenev, you're doing very well indeed.

There was always something childish about Hemingway. He never really grew up. You and I were talking the other day about why one becomes a writer and I thought then about Hemingway's comment, "We're all bitched from the start." He never expanded on that, but we know from the Kenneth Lynn biography and others that he detested his mother and threatened to cut her off financially if she ever gave an interview about him. I don't know what he feared she would say. We do know that she dressed him in girl's dresses until he was three years old—there's a photo of him in a ruffly dress and a big feathered hat labeled by his mother, "My Summer Girl"—and Lynn speculates that this psychic wound, if such it was, became the impetus for the macho element in his writing and in his life. That he felt forced to prove his masculinity in everything he did: fighting, hunting, plowing through a phalanx of women, and of course writing.

Q: *I suppose he wasn't really the tough guy that he pretended to be. He embellished that image.*

JL: At least he cultivated it. But I think he was pretty tough in fact. He survived some terrible injuries. I remember when his plane crashed in the jungle and he walked out of the debris alive, but not before he was declared dead by the newspapers and his obituaries had begun to appear. He sustained massive head injuries and not for the first time. Certainly he was a lot tougher than moi, Miss Piggy here, but it's not a kind of toughness I aspire to. I'm more impressed by the toughness that led him to shoot himself when he realized he could no longer write. I know how that sounds, but when he realized he was no longer able to do the one thing he did well, he offed himself. And I think it took some courage to do that . . . if indeed that's why he did it.

Q: *Could it be that he killed himself because he thought he was a fake and his fakery was about to be exposed?*

JL: Oh! That's so . . . that's so hard on him. He wrote some great prose. He wrote some great stories. He invented a style. He was a very very important writer. Rest in peace, Hemingway, you poor bastard.

Q: *What about poor Maxwell Perkins? He more or less created Hemingway.*

JL: But look what he had to work with. It's true that in a sense he created Hemingway and he did the same for Scott Fitzgerald.

Q: *Fitzgerald helped Hemingway too.*

JL: Yes, he did, he helped him greatly. Therefore, of course, Hemingway turned on him. In *A Moveable Feast* he tries to expose Fitzgerald as having too small a penis to satisfy the needs of Zelda properly. What a friend, what a terrific guy. There was nobody who helped him that he wasn't mean to. What's that famous saying: "Why does he hate me? I never did him a favor." Something like that.

Q: *(Laughs.) That's the first time I've heard it.*

JL: Is that right. It's good, isn't it.

Q: *It's good. On the subject of other writers, last time you mentioned your friendship with Joyce Carol Oates, the dinner and so on. Do you maintain friendships with other writers?*

JL: Joyce is an exceptional case among writers; she has a vast number of writer friends and keeps in touch with all of them; I'm only one of a great many, maybe hundreds. It was she who initiated the friendship actually. I had reviewed her novel, *them*, for *Atlantic* when I was a staff editor there. This was before she was awarded the National Book Award, before she was famous. She wrote and thanked me for the review and said she hoped we might meet sometime. We corresponded for a short while and found we were going to be in London at the same time, so we met there and have been sort of friends ever since. We write Christmas letters, see each other when she comes through Palo Alto. We're not friends in the way Eavan Boland and I are friends, or Ken Fields or Dave MacDonald or Toby Wolff or Ron Hansen. I admire Oates enormously. There hasn't been a writer like her for productivity *cum* quality since Balzac. She's often criticized for writing too much—some years she produces as many as four or five books—but the quality of her writing is right up there with work by people who bring out a book every decade.

My other writer friends are all people at Stanford or people I've taught. I usually maintain friendship with writers from the workshop, though I suppose there are some really distinguished writers who hate me. Jeffrey Eugenides, for instance, who wrote *Middlesex*. I knocked myself out trying to help him; specifically, trying to get him to stop confusing obscurity with profundity. He was convinced, I think, that if you're vague enough, you must be deep. And apparently he got over it somehow and became a fine writer. But as a workshop student he hated the way I went about trying to help him, or maybe he just hated me. He resented my insistence that he was doing injury to his own great talent by holding back all the information we needed to be moved, or informed, or illuminated by a story. But he was a very gifted guy. And the fact is I liked him both as a writer and a person.

Who else? Most of the workshop writers who have become well known remain good friends of mine. I could give you a complete list, but that seems rather silly. Kathryn Harrison, David Hwang, Fenton Johnson, and Michael Cunningham were undergrads when I taught them. And from the graduate workshop, I'll mention a token few, just a few: Harriet Doerr who died not long ago, Stephanie Vaughn, Michael Koch, Ron Hansen, Bo Caldwell, Michelle Carter, Mae Briskin, Allan Gurganus,Toby Wolff, Brent Spencer, these from my early days here. And more recently Keith Scribner, David Vann, Peter Rock, Jason Brown, Samantha Chang, Z.Z. Packer, Josh Tyree, Tom Kealey. There's a long list of distinguished writers, but I'd better just stop here and apologize to friends I've left out.

Q: *Did you ever teach Robert Stone?*

JL: Good God, no. He's nearly my age.

Q: *What do you think of his work?*

JL: I think he's a brilliant writer who's uneven. Even within a single book you can see where he took a break—for a drink or a puff—and then came back, and the writing is all off. It takes him a few pages to gear up again and go on with the book. This is true in *Dog Soldiers* and even in the wonderful *A Flag for Sunrise.* But he remains a fine writer and a superb storyteller.

The problem I find with him is you've got to be of his political or religious persuasion to read him at his best. He presumes on your agreement with his moral stance. There's not that delicate balance you find in a Graham Greene novel or in a book by A. N. Wilson or in any great writer—Tolstoy, for instance, or Chekhov—who also take on issues like suicide, marriage, politics, and war. You have to be a liberal to appreciate Robert Stone fully. I happen to be one but I resent having my good will presumed upon. Does that make sense?

In my own writing I try to let my characters be nasty, commit sin, revel in ugly political stances I don't have. In a novel I've now abandoned, *Casa Sayonara,* there are people who worked for Nixon and who were very close to the seat of power in his administration and afterward. There are also born-again Christians who are waiting for the Final Rapture when we'll all be snatched out of our clothes and the streets will flow with the blood of people whom the avenging Jesus has come to punish. In real life these folks give me the fantods, but in fiction I'm not making fun of them. I make them sincerely believe this stuff. Characters in fiction deserve the independence and integrity we all think we possess in real life. Sorry. That was a pretty messy answer.

Q: *Why do you say you've abandoned it? It sounds pretty lively to me.*

JL: *Atlantic* saw the first draft and they were less than enchanted. So I took it back and did another draft, and then another, and in the end Joan hated all the characters—she found them uninteresting, the worst sin—and I came to doubt the book myself, so it's in the garage waiting for someone to call and ask if I've got anything abandoned in my garage that needs publishing.

Q: *But really . . .*

JL: It's a non-starter and a big disappointment to me. Failure is never pleasant to reminisce about. Is that okay? Are we still friends?

Q: *Okay, let's go back to Robert Stone. I have a different take on his work. I find his language, his writing, to be labored and tortuous. It doesn't flow naturally. I think it lacks grace, and I'm not flattering you but yours is polished, smooth. There is an elegance to it.*

JL: But my language is very simple.

Q: *Yes, it's simple, but it reads nicely.*

JL: Well, that may be because I write out loud. If you say the words as you write them, you immediately hear the difference between what the ear can accept with ease and what it wants to resist.

Q: *Maybe that's the answer. The book I thought succeeded best was his first novel,* The Hall of Mirrors. *It explained America to me in some sense.*

JL: Mm-hmm. I confess it's one of the two Stone books I haven't read. That and *Damascus.*

Q: *I've read them all but I couldn't read* The Gates of Damascus. *I started reading it but I just couldn't get into it.*

JL: I couldn't either. I read about a hundred pages and it seemed very self-indulgent to me, overwrought, careless even. But we haven't read it, so we're disqualified here as critics, the both of us.

Q: *Okay. Let's go back to obscurity being confused with profundity. I couldn't get into* Middlesex *for precisely that reason.*

JL: Really? He holds back information? I haven't read it, though I suppose I should, if only to exorcise the guilt I feel for having pushed him too hard. Or having failed to push him at all.

Q: *I've been very influenced by a booklet by B.R. Myers called* Reader's Manifesto *that I first read in the* Atlantic. *It appeared there as an article in a shorter version. Have you read that?*

JL: No. I've never heard of it. Is it recent?

Q: *A few years ago. He writes about popular books.*

JL: Oh, I should read this.

Q: *He dissects everything.*

JL: It's a book?

Q: *A booklet. Apparently* Atlantic *wanted him to cut it back for the article and he later published it in its entirety as a booklet. I thought it was a pretty daring piece. It takes on work by well-known or established authors including Cormac McCarthy and Don DeLillo and Annie Proulx. Also Paul Auster, I think, and Guterson—*Snow Falling on Cedars. *He quotes a passage at length and then asks "What does this mean?" And he takes it apart.*

JL: A close reading of the text. Line by line.

Q: *And image by image. It's pretty thorough analysis.*

JL: It sounds like my cup of tea. My cup of hemlock. I had this discussion with Toby in a workshop—we were there together in front of the group—and he allowed as how sometimes McCarthy is a bit florid and added, "But would you be willing to sacrifice even one of his sentences." And I said yes, I would. And I cited the opening of *All The Pretty Horses* whose first paragraph leaves the reader lost, now inside and now outside the house. It sets a mood but disorients the reader when really he wants to set the reader down in a tough, concrete world. I couldn't quote the passage, of course, so I made a mess of my protest. Toby, sweet man that he is, was hurt that I would criticize McCarthy in this public way. Mind you, this was before his *No Country for Old Men* and his great novel *The Road.*

Q: *Did Wolff accuse you of nitpicking?*

JL: Toby's too kind to say that, but in fact there is no such thing as nitpicking with language or with the way a narrative proceeds. To which Toby would of course agree. If your prose disorients your reader—because it's too florid or too self-conscious or imprecise—then you should rewrite it. It's that simple.

Q: *Let's move from friends to marriage. One of the first things I heard about you is that for a long time you had a commuting marriage.*

JL: Dear God.

Q: *Do you want to talk about that?*

JL: More than anything in the world. (Laughs.) For 14 years we commuted between Palo Alto and Boston. Joan and I were married in 1971 when I was a staff editor of *Atlantic,* then later I became editor-in-chief of *The Boston Review of the Arts,* and in '73 I got this great job teaching at Stanford. Joan came out and couldn't find a teaching job here—the timing was terrible—and so she returned to her job in Boston. Fortunately we had a long experience of deferred gratification—she had been a nun and I was a priest before we met—and so the marriage held together despite this enormous strain on it. At first people thought this was some Catholic way of breaking up and then after a while, when we were still together, other couples began to think, This is a pretty good way to conduct a marriage, six months on, six months off. I began to sense among some couples a feeling of envy for our strange way of life. But it was in fact very difficult.

Q: *Did it affect your writing?*

JL: I threw all my time into directing the writing program; I became Director in 1976. And during my time off, I wrote. Joan and I got together quite a lot, actually, because I had almost a month free at Christmas, and our winter and spring breaks came at different times, so Joan would come out here during hers and I'd go out there during mine, and of course we had all summer out here together. But it wasn't a conventional marriage. It was always about to be interrupted.

Q: *Tell me about directing the writing program. Did that affect your writing?*

JL: Yes, I suppose it did. I foolishly regarded it as a full-time job. I was in my office before nine and left around six, and none of that time went on my own writing. There was a long period—between 1976 and 1988—when I published only one book, *Desires,* my second collection of stories. And then I stopped being Director and published four books in the next four years—*A Woman Run Mad, Comedians, An Honorable Profession,* and *The Shrine at Altamira.* But there had been that long drought with only one book in eleven years and that's because I was giving all my time to the writing program. "I gave that woman the best years of my life." But I did it willingly.

Q: *What did you get out of it?*

JL: Enormous satisfaction. I liked being Director of this really distinguished program. And I managed to change the composition of the program and make it essentially what it is today. When I took over we had three fellowships in fiction and two in poetry and a wholly inadequate M.A. program. At that time there were lots of other M.A. programs, really good ones, that were offering solid money to promising writers whereas all we could offer them was their tuition, a considerable sum, but not enough to compete with Iowa and Cornell and Hopkins. With a lot of trust from the Dean's office, I managed to drop the M.A. program and use the tuition money to finance further fellowships. And I spent a lot of those eleven years raising money for fellowships so that in the end—as it is today—we had ten full fellowships in fiction and ten in poetry and the Fellows' only obligation is to attend workshop and write the best stuff they can. There's no comparable program in the country today. Everybody gets the same pile of money, the same attention, the same opportunities, with their only obligation being that they write hard and write better. Mind you, it was a very distinguished program when Wally Stegner started it in 1947 and I used to worry that he'd not approve of my dropping the M.A. program, but in fact he sent me a lovely letter saying that I had found it brick and left it gold. A typically generous response from a great writer who, after all, founded the program I'd inherited.

That was the greatest satisfaction of being Director. Also it provided the opportunity to give money to people, give them teaching jobs, introduce them to my connections from *Atlantic*. I got a lot of satisfaction from that. I probably could have been a better writer if I'd done less administrative work, but I don't regret it.

Q: *You say you could have been a better writer.*

JL: More prolific.

Q: *Better, you said. Is there a moment—I'm guessing that there is—is there a moment when a writer realizes that, yes, I can push forward into deeper territory? And if there is, is there also a moment—sad, I would think, and difficult—when the writer realizes that this is it, I can't go any further?*

JL: Mm-hmm.

Q: *I've gone as far as I can go.*

JL: I'm slow in responding, but I do know what you're talking about. I think Flannery O'Connor, when she was very near death and turning out her last and greatest stories, found herself heartbroken that she couldn't go on to another novel. But I think she was mistaken. I think she had taken her material and her magnificent control of it as far as it would go in those last great stories "The Partridge Festival" and "Revelation" and "Parker's Back." She would have been repeating herself. Her new work would be only a variation on what she had already done; it wouldn't have been any broader or deeper.

In a small way—and I don't for a second mean to compare myself to the great Flannery O'Connor—I think that happened to me with a certain kind of material. Specifically, with the way God meddles in our lives to call our attention away from ourselves to something larger than ourselves. This is a theme I explore in *Jessica Fayer* and explore again in a larger way in *A Woman Run Mad* and you can see it reappearing in different forms in *Comedians* and *An Honorable Profession* and *The Shrine at Altamira.* In each of these books God gets in the way of our lives as we'd prefer to live them. After *Shrine* there was no way I could take this idea any farther. So I took a deep breath and moved into a more easily recognizable world. I went back to satire and *The Handmaid of Desire.* And after *Handmaid, Having Everything.* In my abandoned novel, *Casa Sayonara,* I was working in a very contemporary, post-Christian society . . . where, I confess, I'm not at my most comfortable as a writer. Maybe that was the problem.

Q: *A post-Christian society. Do you believe in God? Well, obviously you do.*

JL: Something like that.

Q: *Do you say to yourself, "I believe in God," or "God is not Robertson's or Jerry Falwell's God."*

JL: Okay, let's deal with it head on. After our previous interview I knew this question was coming and so I dug out a little notebook entry I made in Venice some years ago. We were spending a month there as we often do, and when we're in Venice Joan and I go to mass every day. I almost never go to mass here in Palo Alto, though there's never a day that I don't worry about what it is I actually believe, and why . . . especially now that I'm easing toward death. Well, on this particular day—12 December 2001—I decided to think it through by writing it down. I planned to start at the beginning to see if I could discover how I got to where I am now, spiritually, theologically. This is what I wrote:

> "When I was nineteen I believed passionately in a life beyond this one. Not an afterlife—I never gave thought to an afterlife—but a life of honesty, selflessness, a life of perfection I equated somehow with a living death. I remember explaining to my mother, with satisfaction and what passed for joy, that in the monastery I would be 'legally dead.'
>
> "I applied for admission to the Jesuits, I was accepted, and at 21 I took vows of poverty, chastity, and obedience. I wasn't 'legally dead' of course. I was a pious bore, with romantic ideas and a frightening will power. I remained a Jesuit for 17 years, was ordained, said Mass, heard confessions. Love? Jesus? What sustained me? I shudder to think.
>
> "At 67, married now for 30 years, I attend daily Mass in Venice at the Church of San Trovaso. I join the little community in reciting Matins, receiving communion, exchanging the kiss of peace. I am with my wife, always, the one person who gives shape and meaning to my life. She is one of God's intimates. I am not. I am an outsider, an observer, a spy at the feast."

Q: *And?*

JL: That was as far as I got because I couldn't answer any of the questions about what I believe and why. I couldn't even frame them properly. Of course I believe in God, whatever that means. Of course I believe in sin: I think there are two sins: the sin against charity and the sin against justice. I don't think the Church should ever have gotten into the sex business or the business of identifying sins by kind and number. Charity and justice cover everything that's right or wrong. In adultery, you sin against a third party by being unjust and uncharitable both. In fornication you may hurt nobody, unless you're just using them for sex, and if so you're sinning against charity. In masturbation—the great teen bugaboo—it's hard to imagine sin at all. I remember a moral theologian saying in class, "It's hard to imagine Jesus caring what a teenager does with his winkler." Jesus does care, I think, about a just wage, an honest day's work, the ugliness of hypocrisy, our treatment of the poor, the sick, the dying, the prisoner. These are matters of justice. Charity and justice cover it all, I think, and I wish the Church had never begun legislating on sex. But these aren't questions I think about much; I've made up my mind on them.

What I worry about every day is what I believe and why, and I simply can't say.

Q: *What about Heaven and Hell?*

JL: Wouldn't it be nice. I like what Schopenhauer says about death. "Death is that long sleep in which individuality is forgotten." That's a kind of grim comfort. It's not terribly different from what the priest says in the mass for the dead: "Lord, grant them eternal rest." He doesn't add anything about green pastures and bright lights.

Q: *You don't sound like a very orthodox Catholic.*

JL: No, but we can always hope that a lifetime spent as a Catholic has left me believing more than I know. Or at least full of hope.

Q: *One of your characters in* The Miracle, *Father Moriarty, is given to saying, "God . . . if there is a God . . . " Can we conclude that Father Moriarty is you?*

JL: If only! Father Moriarty is a saint. He's got a foul tongue and he's short-tempered and a frightening wit, but he's experiencing what the great Saint Teresa experienced, the Dark Night of the Soul, in which all human consolation is denied him. Furthermore he is in constant pain—he's dying of ALS—and it's his perverse amusement to express as a joke what he fears deep in his heart: maybe there is no God. But he goes on—loving, in his way—straight to the end.

Q: *Shall we end this now, on a nice positive note?*

JL: Amen.

INTERVIEW 4

Q: *To change the subject, let's talk about movies today. I understand you like movies.*

JL: I like movies a lot, but I came to them very late in life. My ignorance of movies is practically un-American.

Q: *I thought everybody grew up with movies. No?*

JL: I grew up in a tiny town, South Hadley, Massachusetts. There were no theatres in town. You had to go to the town across the river, Holyoke, where there were three little theatres. I only went for major film events, like "Ali Baba and the Forty Thieves." But I missed all the shoot-em-ups and the westerns and the serials that everybody my age saw.

Q: *Tell me why you didn't see them. You said everyone else did.*

JL: Oh, I see, you're after my tragic youth. The fact is I was four years younger than my brother and there were no other kids my age in my neighborhood, so there was nobody to go to movies with. Until I was seven years old Billy Muir was my friend; he was my age exactly and he lived four houses down from me. But at seven Billy moved to Chicago and the family soon became very rich. Three years later his father committed suicide after he was thrown in jail for embezzlement and I never heard from Billy Muir again. So for all those years—from age seven to fourteen—I was my own playmate. I read books morning, noon, and night. Sometimes I'd walk up to the school grounds—a long hike—on Saturdays to play softball, but for most of the time I was on my own. Actually I was quite content with my books.

But you should tell me about movies. You grew up in Syria—Damascus, right?—with millions of friends to hang out with. In a culture that loved movies. And the theatres were just around the corner from you.

Q: *It was a little like Holyoke. There were half a dozen theatres that showed mostly American movies. I guess I went to the movies a lot because at the Armenian elementary school I went to in Damascus we were forbidden to see movies.*

JL: On the grounds that they were corrupting?

Q: *I assume so. We were never told why. But somehow corruption didn't occur to me as the reason. I think it was something like the belief that movies led to idleness, laziness, and it was a waste of time to sit in the dark for two hours when you could be doing your homework, helping your father, contributing to the support of your family.*

JL: In an earlier age, it would have been reading novels that wasted time and gave you the wrong ideas about life.

Q: *I think so.*

JL: *Madame Bovary*. Emma begins to go astray when she gets all these false romantic notions from reading fiction.

Q: *Back to you. You start going to the movies in some serious way at what stage in your life?*

JL: I don't think I ever did, you see, because I went away to college for two years and then into the Jesuits where we had no movies—in fact we had no radio or television and, for the first four years, no newspapers—so I'd be about thirty, I guess, before I went to movies the way normal people do. Mind you, I like movies. Film is a great art form and one that's interesting to me. I'd love to write a movie, but as you can see I'm woefully unequipped.

Q: *Why?*

JL: Precisely because it is an art form, and you have to learn to write it the way you have to learn to write fiction. I was asked by the producer Scott Rudin if I wanted to write the script for *A Woman Run Mad* and I said no immediately because I knew it would involve a huge investment of my time in a form I knew nothing about.

Q: *Let me ask one more question about movies. Do they influence your imagination?*

JL: I suppose they do, some. Less than fiction.

Q: *Would I be guessing correctly in saying that influence is minimal because you were not exposed extensively to movies during your formative years?*

JL: Influence aside, I always write as if the scene I'm writing is meant to be filmed. Not because I'm trying to write a film but because I want the reader to see it the way I see it, as a series of images unfolding in front of me. That's why Hollywood people sometimes option my books for movies. *The Shrine at Altamira,* if you can believe it, was bought twice for movies, a book that could never in a million years become a successful film. Each scene is sufficiently vivid and could be filmed just as it is, but the film would be too horrifying to look at.

Q: *Is this the book that was optioned by Scott Rudin?*

JL: No. The first time, it was optioned by Richard LeGravanese who wrote *The Fisher King,* which I didn't see, but I understand he got the Academy Award for his script. The second option was by James Woods, the actor, who wanted to play the father in it. And direct it. Rudin's only interest has been in *A Woman Run Mad.*

Q: *I remember reading in the Stanford Daily that you had signed a contract with Rudin for a small fortune. I'd like to hear the story.*

JL: By today's standards, small indeed. But it was kind of interesting and says something about how Hollywood works. What happened is that *A Woman Run Mad* appeared to a lot of hot reviews and right away the film people began to express interest. Rudin offered a $50,000 option against a final payment of $250,000 on the first day of filming. Suddenly Roman Polanski phoned my agent from France to say he wanted the book shipped to him by overnight mail. Word got out and Rudin told my agent that he would raise the price to $350,000 if I signed before Monday. This was a Saturday and—no fool, moi—I said yes at once. And this has happened with Rudin three separate times. He pays me the option money, hires a screenwriter to do a screenplay—for a cool million, I suspect—and when it's done he rejects it as inadequate, and then the rights revert to me once more. And I've sold it subsequently to Tom Reed at Highwire Productions—again, no screenplay—and it's under consideration now by Costigan, who just directed "Brokeback Mountain."

Q: *So it's done well for you,* A Woman Run Mad.

JL: Movie money is the best money because it droppeth as the gentle dew from heaven. You don't share it with anybody. Your agent gets fifteen percent, as he should, but it's not like dealing with a publisher, where you split half. If you get $500,000 for a paperback sale—like Allan Gurganus for *Oldest Living Confederate Widow Tells All*—you get only $250,000, and your agent gets fifteen percent of that, and then the state and federal tax people get nearly half of that. So you end up with about $125,000 out of your original $500,000. Go with the movies, I say. Buy a house.

Q: *Speaking of agents, you have two agents. One for the movies, down in Hollywood, and the other one in New York?*

JL: Right.

Q: *How long have you worked with them?*

JL: I've only had one Hollywood agent. I had him because he was an arm of my New York agent, and then they split off and I just stayed with him for movies. The way Hollywood works is essentially a mystery.

New York is another matter; I have some understanding of what a New York agent does and how he does it. Like most writers my age, I've had many New York agents over the years. I've had the odd experience—twice, actually—of being represented by an agent who became phenomenally rich because of some mega-deal she struck and who then had little time or interest in representing me. And it's understandable. If you're making deals in the millions and taking ten or fifteen percent of the total, why would you want to spend time on somebody who gets a $10,000 advance? At one point I had an agent who had Kurt Vonnegut and Mike Nichols as clients, so obviously he wasn't going to pay as much attention to me as to these guys. I've been with my current agent, Peter Matson, for about ten years. He's very good. We get along well.

Q: *How did you get your first agent?*

JL: Actually, I didn't have an agent at all until my sixth book. My first five books were all sold by me directly to the publishers: Doubleday first, then Macmillan. That's unimaginable today because you'd never be able to get an editor to look at your manuscript. I had an advantage: my first four books were poetry and I had published a lot in *Atlantic* and other good places so that gave me a small entree, I suppose. *Picnic in Babylon*—a journal before journals became a fashion—was sold to Macmillan, again without an agent. It made a lot of money, which quite rightly went to the Jesuits. Now that I think of it, I sold my first novel, *Tight White Collar,* without an agent, so that makes six books on my own. Then somebody told me I had to have an agent to protect subsidiary rights, paperbacks, and movies, etc. So I looked around and found my first agent. This was in the '60s. It was easier then.

Q: *What do you think about the current state of publishing? At one time an editor worked closely with writers from the start and the publishing firm itself would . . .*

JL: . . . would commit to them. I know.

Q: *. . . commit to them and refine or polish the manuscript.*

JL: Right. Maxwell Perkins is the archetypal example of the great editor.

Q: *He helped fix* The Sun Also Rises.

JL: And Wolfe's *Look Homeward, Angel,* and all those others.

Q: *Now this work is passed on to agents.*

JL: Part of it to agents, but most of it to writing programs. That's really the function of workshops today. We teach, yes, but in large part we've replaced literary editors. We help teach writers how to edit their own work.

Q: *So, ultimately, when they submit a manuscript . . .*

JL: It's pretty much complete.

Q: *. . . be it to the agent or to the publisher, it's done, so that the publisher has no heavy editing left to do.*

JL: I've heard of only one agent, ever, who actually sends back the book manuscript and says, "Look, this needs work in these particular areas." Keith Scribner, no relation to the publisher, has an agent who did that with his first novel, *The GoodLife,* with no space between "Good" and "Life." Agents are people who love writing but who mostly don't do it themselves. Or people who were editors and just got tired of working in the trenches and decided to go make some money off other people's work. But they are generally not as literarily accomplished as the writers they market. It's a similar case with editors. Very often editors can't—or at least they don't—write themselves but they have a very good sense of what will sell. Mind you, the higher up the ladder you go, the more accomplished and effective the editors become. I don't want to sound as if I think agents and editors are merely a nuisance that stands between the writer and the published book. They're smart people, they do important work. But I tend to trust the writer more when it comes to a question of what he's actually doing.

You know, you were talking about how publishers used to commit to writers and publish their books even when one came along that they didn't like and thought might not sell well. I'm thinking of Edith Wharton here. Her publisher had made a lifetime commitment to her and, even though they really disliked one of her books and thought it inferior to her usual work, they went ahead and published it. And, if I recall correctly, they were right: it wasn't up to her best work and it did not sell well. But they stood by her. That kind of thing is gone forever. Now as soon as you don't sell, they drop you. This happened recently to a friend of mine, a major writer, whose every book had been published by Random House, and whose new novel they decided wasn't going to sell well, so they canned her. This same thing happened to me at Viking Penguin. My editor got fired after eighteen years with the firm and the editor who replaced her wanted to clear her desk and so she got rid of me along with everybody else on the editor's list, unless they were producing major revenue. I was just another expense she could take off the balance sheet.

This works in two ways of course. With no loyalty to the writer on the publisher's part, the writer returns the favor: he knows he'll be dumped as soon as he doesn't make money and so he'll move to some other publisher as soon as he gets a better offer. It happens every day. Guterson, for instance, after *Snow Falling on Cedars* and Charles Frazier after *Cold Mountain.* The bottom line is money. So I'm very lucky that after 17 books I'm still published at all . . . especially since my books stopped making any real money after *Shrine at Altamira.*

Q: *Well, your books sell well enough . . .*

JL: To appear in the black column on the account sheet, but that's not really enough any more.

Q: *Could you talk a little bit about your recent books, how they've performed? They've all been issued in paperback.*

JL: Right, but by the same companies that published them. So I don't know if that means anything particularly. But Atlantic Monthly Press is a very good press and they publish me because they believe in publishing serious literature and they're nice enough to think that's what I write. *The Miracle,* for instance, which is my most recent book.

Q: *That's also been released in paperback.*

JL: Right. And it sold pretty well. The advance was tiny--$6,000—and I used to get as much as $70,000, regularly, following *A Woman Run Mad.* Ah, the old days. Of course I did get royalties for *The Miracle* in addition to my $6,000, but not as much as you'd think; a few thousand only. And that's after it won the gold medal in the California Book Awards. But Atlantic Monthly Press is not an ordinary publishing house; they take a chance on books that they know won't be best sellers. Scribners, for instance, wanted to publish *Having Everything* but turned it down because their marketing department couldn't guarantee a minimal sale of 35,000 copies.

Publishing today is in a grim situation, especially if you've published a number of books and haven't earned your publisher a lot of money. It's very embarrassing in your old age to be crippled in this particular way. On the other hand, 17 books is a good record, and if this new book doesn't sell, I'll probably go on and write the next one. We've got a good-sized garage for storing manuscripts.

Q: *Let's talk about your next book. It's completed, I understand, or at least you've got a first draft.*

JL: This version—the first draft—is finished, and I'm more or less pleased with it, but I'm reluctant to say it's near completion because the last couple of books have gone through three different versions. But I'm comfortable enough with it to talk about it, so if you've got questions, I'll pretend to answer them.

Q: *Well, you've said it's about obsession, a subject you've dealt with before—I'm thinking of* A Woman Run Mad *and* The Shrine at Altamira*—and I wonder how you came to link Donatello with obsession.*

JL: Okay, good. Way back in 1999 on my first trip to Florence I had the good fortune to visit the Accademia and the Bargello on the same day, which meant I got to see Michelangelo's David in the morning and Donatello's David in the afternoon. This provided me with a good close-up contrast. I was astonished at the Michelangelo—it's vast and overwhelming—and I was embarrassed by the Donatello. I didn't know where to look. The statue is so unashamedly naked. And erotic, with an eroticism that is quite calculated, I think. It asks to be looked at. It asks to be touched. I knew absolutely nothing about Donatello at that time, but one look at the David convinced me that Donatello knew exactly what he was doing and went ahead and did it anyway.

Q: *And you knew this how?*

JL: Instinct. Intuition. I was convinced that Donatello was recording the moment of his seduction. Memorializing it for posterity.

Q: *Isn't that quite a leap, from a single look to a firm conviction?*

JL: Yes, no doubt about it. But as I looked around the Bargello—almost the entire second floor is given over to sculptures by Donatello—I could see that the David is unique. All the other men look like men, solid, Old Testament figures in the case of his great prophet series, and noble, virile, capable men in his random figures of Saint George, Saint Louis, Saint Antony. Even his earlier David, in marble, looks manly . . . saintly, but manly. The bronze David is absolutely unique. It looks more like a pre-pubescent girl than like the shepherd boy who felled Goliath with a slingshot.

Q: *You've done research on this, of course. Does the research bear out your conclusion? As a matter of fact what is your conclusion?*

JL: About the statue, you mean, and its relation to Donatello?

Q: *If that's what you're getting at.*

JL: I concluded first that there's a story here. That whoever modeled for this David meant more to Donatello personally than the models for Saint George or Saint Louis. Donatello gives the statue an audacity, a sexual defiance, that I'm sure he captured from the model. It's not superimposed. It's there in the boy posing for him. And their relationship, I concluded, was by its nature designed to break his heart.

Q: *Was Donatello homosexual?*

JL: His contemporaries joked about his habit of hiring only pretty boys as his assistants and of course assistants very often served as models. There are about seven extant stories of Donatello at work and at play, and at least two of them concern his attachment to good-looking boys. It wasn't that rare a thing among Renaissance artists. Ghiberti and DaVinci and Michelangelo were practicing homosexuals even though sodomy was punishable by burning at the stake. And people were actually punished this way. In 1429, just before Donatello sculpted his bronze boy, Piero di Jacopo was burned at the stake for sodomy. In Florence. So messing around with one of your assistants could be a very dangerous thing as Donatello was well aware. Art historians today—Janson and Pope-Hennessy, for instance—pretty much agree that the statue is a commemoration of homosexual eroticism.

Q: *So this boy enters Donatello's life and, I gather, changes it for good. Is he the first person narrator you mentioned?*

JL: Actually no. The first person narrator is a failed sculptor who observes the relationship from start to finish and like all good first person narrators he's a snoop and a confidant. He sees everything, and whatever he can't know for certain, he manages to elicit from people who do know.

Let me back up a moment. The narrator is the illegitimate son of a successful merchant who gives him away to a wool dyer and then later reclaims him and forces him into the Franciscans. He fails as a Franciscan—he's thrown out for various good reasons—and then he's indentured to an artist, Cennino Cennini, and from there he moves on to

Ghiberti and from Ghiberti to Donatello. He fails at everything he does, but he has charm and good looks and, salvifically, a skill with numbers and so he becomes Donatello's bookkeeper, accountant, and confidant. The perfect position for a spy.

Q: *It sounds as if you must have done a lot of research for this book.*

JL: Actually research for this thing is an endless process. I never really intended to write the book even though I began keeping notes for it as early as 1999. I thought of it as a project for my old age, something I could keep noodling away at right up to the moment of my death . . . or my being sent doddering and drooling to *Casa Sayonara* . . . and when people would ask, "Are you working on a new book?" I would reply, "Oh yes, a long term project on Donatello." And then I'd leave a pile of notes and nothing more at my death, but I'd have been able to kid myself that I was still at work.

Q: *That's really planning ahead.*

JL: Well, I was writing the doomed *Casa Sayonara* at this time, remember, so my research was really quite remote. And a lot of fun. Joan and I took three courses from Christy Junkerman on the painting and sculpture of Renaissance Florence, Venice, and Rome. We studied Italian and began spending every Christmas and summer in Venice. And I got deep into Medici history and the Black Plague and the art and craft of sculpting. So it was a great way to use up time without actually sitting in front of a computer. All this so-called research was remote, as I say, because it's deep background and what I learned should be so much part of the text that it's not noticeable on the surface. Research should never stick out, I mean. You should be so lost in the world of Florence, 1435, that you fail to notice that any research went into the fabric of the text.

Q: *It sounds like a daunting project.*

JL: It was. It is. I would never have put a word on paper—notes don't count—except that I got a Guggenheim Fellowship in

2006. Earlier that year the Dean asked if I would like to apply for an Emeritus Mellon Fellowship, which sounded good to me, free money, so I wrote up a proposal for a novel set in the bottega of Donatello but less than a week later I was told the Mellon people had no interest in fiction writing. So much for the Mellon. That same week, however, I got a Guggenheim flyer in the mail, with an application form attached, and I used the Mellon proposal to apply for a Guggenheim. Incredibly, I got a Fellowship. And that's what pushed me from thinking "someday I might write this novel" to "now I've got to begin writing this novel." It's a point of honor. You take the money, you do the job.

Q: *I heard you had gotten a Guggenheim. The only one at Stanford that year.*

JL: Yes, that's why they kept it quiet. Berkeley got ten.

Q: *And you used the money for research?*

JL: Yes, we spent a summer in Florence, wearing out our shoes trekking from church to church, museum to museum. It was glorious.

Q: *What's the oddest thing you've discovered in your research?*

JL: The odd things you discover are things you would never have gone looking for except for the exigencies of plot and character. An example. My first person narrator during his Franciscan period—before he's thrown out of the order—is seduced by the local prostitute who tells him he's much too pretty to be a monk. She undresses him but, as she did so, I realized I had no idea what a Franciscan would be wearing underneath his habit. So I had to go track it down, and in a book on medieval clothing I discovered that he'd be wearing baggy underdrawers held up by a string around his waist. More remarkable still, I discovered that only Franciscans wore underclothes. Dominicans and Benedictines did not. No amount of general research would have elicited this odd and largely useless fact.

Q: *The other orders didn't wear underclothes?*

JL: You can always tell yourself there must have been exceptions. As I'm sure there were.

Q: *What else are you willing to tell me about the novel?*

JL: Well, let's see. It's built upon the historical framework of events from the first half of the fifteenth century in Florence. Its precise background is the struggle between the Medici and the Albizzi for the control of Florence. The foreground is occupied by the events in Donatello's bottega as he sets about—with enormous difficulty—sculpting his bronze David. Which is, by the way, the first free-standing nude bronze in over a thousand years. Donatello really did change the history of sculpture in the early Renaissance. DaVinci and Michelangelo learned a great deal from his work.

Q: *Do you feel you know Donatello intimately now?*

JL: I wish I could say yes, but the nature of his genius is so complicated, so mysterious, that the best I can do is try to draw a circle around the mystery, and tighten that circle, and keep tightening it until I can say, yes, this is precisely what I do not understand. It's a mystery that can be felt even if it can't be fully explained. I know him and I don't know him. He was a lovely, loving human being, the soul of generosity, given to outbursts of rage, funny and sly and gifted beyond measure. Like the rest of humanity, only bigger and better.

Q: *Anything more?*

JL: I've already said a great deal too much. I'll regret this one day.

Q: *Why would that be? Why do you say that?*

JL: I'm thinking of *Casa Sayonara.* What if *The Bronze Boy* should go the way of *Casa* and turn out to be a non-starter? Would I have the courage to go on to another book?

Q: *As a matter of fact what would you do?*

JL: Well, perhaps I'd go back to a play I wrote ten years ago.

Actually it was a two-parter, two one-acts. The first was a dramatization of my story, "Consolations of Philosophy," and the second was to be called "The Philosophy of Consolation." And the total bill would be "A Terrible Evening with John L'Heureux." You can already see the reviews, can't you: "A terrible Evening with John L'Heureux. It is."

A few years ago I went back and looked at the first play and found it very funny and painful and, I think, not bad. It was a lot more fun than I remembered and I was sufficiently encouraged to turn it into a full-length hundred-minute play. Short, but long enough to stand alone. I submitted it to a play contest at the Lord Leebrick Theatre Company in Eugene, Oregon, and it was chosen as a finalist. Alas, the ultimate judgment on it was not good. Mind you, I loved what they said. "It moves well—with something like the head-shaking fascination of "What The Butler Saw." It has merits in diction and in its suitability for our audience, but the treatment of the subject matter verges on the barbarous." I love that, "verges on the barbarous." And it does. They got it, perfectly. And they were very generous in bothering to send me their response.

I'd like to go back to the play sometime and add a scene that's been buzzing in my head ever since I abandoned *Casa.* It's a good, ugly scene that would make the play even more barbarous.

Q: *Watching you talk I wonder if you have ever thought of acting?*

JL: From the time I was a kid, I was interested in theatre and wanted very much to be an actor. I saved up $500 to go to the National Academy of Theatre Arts for a summer straight out of high school. My parents were horrified. They consulted my aunt who was a nun and she said let him do it. It's only for a summer and he'll get it out of his blood. I acted for two summers in stock while I was at college and I acted in a play on television, then I entered the Jesuits and never acted again. Though some would say I act all the time.

Q: *(Laughs.) You were in the Jesuits for seventeen years.*

JL: Just seventeen. (Laughs.)

Q: *We'll have to come back to that. You seem to have a number of projects under way at the same time. How do you keep them straight? Do you take notes?*

JL: Sure. I have a notebook always. After I had published my first few books of poetry, Howard Gotlieb at Boston University wrote and said he wanted to have my personal papers for B.U. Special Collections. Astonishing. I didn't know then that he asked for the papers of everybody who published anything. I was just one among hundreds. Anyhow he pointed out that correspondence and first drafts are valuable but the most valuable thing is your notebook. I had kept a notebook for years and indeed, published it—*Picnic in Babylon, A Jesuit Priest's Journal*—so I wasn't new to the idea, or fond of it either, but a notebook turned out to be a very useful tool for me. Not just in keeping projects straight, but in its function as a confidant. That is, it allows you to talk about your work, about where a scene can go or what a character can become, without dissipating any of the energy that would be lost in actually talking about it. It allows you to test possibilities, to raise questions, to doubt yourself . . . and to do so without becoming a world-class bore or, worse, somebody who talks away his work instead of writing it. I've found that I often work out the solution to a writing problem by talking it through on paper. It's a strange phenomenon. It's not the same as thinking. It's a much slower kind of thing because you're moving your hand across the page and testing the right and wrong of a proposition as you mull it in your mind. I have a notebook for each novel I've written.

Q: *So there's not just one notebook?*

JL: "Deep Thoughts by John L'Heureux"? No. These are all practical—or practice—notebooks and never meant to be read by anybody. But they were useful to me.

Q: *And you're leaving these to Boston University? Not to Stanford?*

JL: Stanford has all the papers that concern my thirteen years as Director of the Writing Program. It also has the drafts of most of my books and stories. Nobody has seen my notebooks, not even Joan, and I don't think they'd be interesting to anybody except perhaps another writer who is frustrated and anguished and not ready to call it quits. In any case I've decided that whoever sends me off to the crematorium can decide how to dispose of the notebooks. With that cheery thought, shall we end this session?

INTERVIEW 5

Q: *Let's talk today about teaching writing. At what stage do you feel you can detect talent among your students?*

JL: Actually we feel they have talent, quite a lot of it, when we choose them for Fellowships to the graduate workshop. We get between 900 and 1,000 applications each year for a total of five Fellowships, so we'd be very remiss if we chose people who weren't talented. You know how it works. They spend two years in workshop, so there's always a class rotating in as the one ahead rotates out, giving us ten writers in each fiction workshop. It's the same in poetry. Some of the people we choose as Fellows have never published at all, some have published quite a lot, but wherever they are in their career, we like to think we can offer them something besides time and money. We help them become better at what they do, we help them identify more clearly their voice and vision.

Q: *Choosing them can't be easy. How do you narrow down a thousand applications to your final choice of five? It seems almost impossible to do.*

JL: Well, it couldn't be done without David MacDonald. He's a former Fellow himself, and a superb writer. His most recent novel—*Lauchlin of the Bad Heart*—is his best, I think. It's about an ex-boxer whose heart may have given out in some respects but not in any that really matter. It's a deeply felt and very moving novel. It's superb, really. So we're lucky to have a first class writer who is willing to do this. Think of it. Each year he reads and writes comments on every last manuscript, getting the finalists down to fifty or sixty. I don't know how Dave has the fortitude for it. No bad heart there, I'll tell you. I've read as many as 400 when I was Director and I found it absolutely killing, but Dave reads the entire pile of them every year. And continues to write great stuff.

Q: *Who chooses the final five?*

JL: We all do, the whole committee: Dave Mac, Toby Wolff, Elizabeth Tallent, and me. The three of us who teach the graduate workshop, plus Dave.

Q: *Interesting. How much does the promise of success have to do with the writers you choose?*

JL: It depends on what you mean by success. Good writing that few people read, good writing that a lot of people read, good writing that makes the writer a household name: these are three varieties of success. Brent Spencer is read by few people, but he's a superb writer with a discerning audience. Alice Hoffman has a large body of readers, devoted fans, and she's very well reviewed. Scott Turow is a household name, a best seller, a great talent. To my way of thinking each of these writers is successful . . . and all of them were in the Stanford workshop.

Q: *Did you teach them all?*

JL: I taught Brent and Alice but not Scott, though he was a lecturer here when I first arrived in '73. He was about to go off to Harvard Law and I remember thinking, that's the loss of a fine talent. I should have realized that law school would give him his great subject.

Q: *I'll come back to Scott Turow later but right now I want to know more about how you spot a writer who hasn't yet found his voice and vision.*

JL: I don't think you can ever be sure who's going to make the most of his or her raw talent. A lot of people have talent and don't become successful writers and then again some writers make it big without any talent you can notice; they succeed on will power and a catchy subject matter. Haven't we talked about this in an earlier interview?

Anyhow, after all these years of dealing with writers and writing, I think I've developed a kind of instinct. I have the feeling periodically—even among undergraduates who have yet to produce much of anything—that this kid's got the talent to write and, most important, the endurance to stick with it. I remember thinking exactly that years ago when I taught Kathryn Harrison, then an undergraduate and now a quite famous writer. She's written *Thicker Than Water, Exposed, The Binding Chair,* and—infamously—*The Kiss,* about her relations with her father, a brave and tragic book. She stood out because she wrote intensely and privately, her work was unlike that of anyone else in her class, and she clearly had a dark well of experience to draw upon. She was also spectacularly beautiful, but that was irrelevant.

There were a couple other undergrads I was similarly impressed by. One was Michael Cunningham who got the Pulitzer a couple years ago for *The Hours.* He was having a terrible time finishing a story; everything he began went off on some crazy tangent and he just froze. One day I suggested that he forget about stories and just use the rest of the quarter to start a novel. I'd never done that before, or since, but I suppose I was remembering George Green, my freshman English teacher at Holy Cross, who out of nowhere said to me, "This class is a waste of your time. Why don't you write a play instead?" He knew nothing about me, he had no idea of my interest in theatre, he just made this suggestion. I wrote the play and it was produced on local television—no big deal, it was 1953, in Worcester, Massachusetts—and a year later I packed myself off to the Jesuits. But George Green left me with the idea that giving somebody a reprieve from class requirements might be a good thing to do. So I did it with Cunningham.

In that same class there was another very gifted writer, Donna Lee, who has written nothing subsequently, but she had enormous talent. If you had asked me then who in that group would be a "successful" writer, I'd have said Donna Lee, providing she can just get her act together. She was a wild child of the early '70s. She once came to class wearing only a silk slip and army boots, with a string of Raggedy Ann dolls around her neck. No kidding. She was a work of art in progress. She did get her act together and, after a year living on the beach in Hawaii, she went to med school and today she's a practicing physician in Boston. She remains a close friend of Cunningham, by the way. Fenton Johnson was in that class too. He later went to the Iowa Writers Program and then came back here as a Stegner Fellow. He's written some remarkable stuff.

Another undergraduate I taught—well, I taught him very little; he did it all himself, really—was David Hwang, the playwright who wrote *M. Butterfly.* If I may interrupt myself here, I'm beginning to see that the common denominator among the very successful people I've taught is that I've really taught them very little; mostly I've served as a rooting section for them. Anyhow, back to David. He showed up in my office one day and asked me, since I taught drama, to give him a tutorial in playwriting. I asked him to show me what he'd written and it turned out he had nothing to show, only the desire to write plays. It turned out further that he had seen his high school productions but no professional theatre whatsoever. I assured him a tutorial was out of the question but I'd let him take my Intro to Drama class and instead of a term paper he could write a play. I then gave him an armload of plays by Sam Shepard—he was interested, like Shepard, in music—and a pile of other books I wasn't using and I sent him off to read. After the first week of my drama course, he handed me a one-act play he had written, and it was pretty good. I made a few suggestions about dialogue and conflict and I figured that was that. But two weeks later he came back with another play, much better, more sophisticated, and after that . . . *le déluge.* He just kept on writing plays. I gave him two, maybe three, tutorials and the next thing I knew he was off to Yale Drama where, in his first year, he had two plays produced in New York. I had nothing to do with his success. *M. Butterfly* won the Tony Award in 1988 and, I think, the New York Drama Desk Award, and the John Gassner Award for new playwrights. David was a natural, with a work ethic to die for and with the gods of drama pushing him forward. He remains a good friend.

Q: *And all these were undergraduates. Are there any undergraduates right now whose work we should look for in a decade or so?*

JL: Yes, his name is Teddy Steinkellner—he's a Junior—and I'm doing whatever I can not to interfere with his raw talent.

Q: *Steinkellner. Okay. Let's talk about some of your graduate workshop writers.*

JL: Sure. Anybody in particular?

Q: *I know Katharine Andres and I know she loved your workshop.*

JL: Katharine was one of those unusual people who are extraordinarily gifted but who feel little compulsion to write. While she was still in Bennington she published a story in *New Yorker,* a remarkable piece I still remember called "At the Potters," and the first story she wrote in workshop was also published in *New Yorker.* And, I recall, she was embarked on a marvelous novel that reminded me of Elizabeth Bowen's *The House in Paris* for its uncanny ability to see adult life through the eyes of a precocious child. She taught here after her fellowship ended and then she began to have babies and she put the novel aside. But she'll write again, I'm sure. It's in the family: her grandfather was Gilbert Seldes, her mother is Marian Seldes, the actress, and her uncle is Tim Seldes, the writer and agent. Sheer family feeling will force her back to writing, I think.

Q: *What about Eugenides and his problem with obscurity.*

JL: We've talked about him already; he's not the only one with that problem.

Q: *So is this problem of deliberate obscurity a common one?*

JL: I suppose we should establish at once that obscurity can sometimes be a good thing. I have nothing against holding back information that the reader doesn't need. Think of Hemingway who made it a method in his short fiction. That kind of deliberate reticence can enhance the reader's experience by forcing him to cooperate imaginatively in rounding out character or event, though of course a lot depends on the sophistication of the reader and the murkiness of the writer.

The obscurity I rail against is the deliberate withholding of information that's necessary to complete the emotional or intellectual experience of the story, either because the writer won't tell you or doesn't himself know. Let me give a practical example. To say "I don't know what this means" about a passage in Faulkner is very different from saying "I don't know what this means," about a passage in a story being workshopped. The burden of literary history is on Faulkner's side and so it's up to the reader to look for clarification in the text itself. But in a workshop where you're dealing with a story-in-progress, it's not unreasonable to say, "I don't understand this passage; can you explain what you mean? " And if the writer answers, "I'm not sure" or "I haven't decided," you know there's a problem.

Young writers conceal information for what seems to them at the time to be a good reason; usually because they think the refusal of information will be stunning . . . as if it were up to the reader to complete the story. Often they do it to induce horror. I recall a workshop story that ended with the search for a missing teenager, and when the body was found in a cave by the sea, the girl who found it backed away from the sight screaming, "No, no, it's too horrible to look at! No human being could do such a thing!" The end. And the reader is left to speculate on what unspeakable horror the girl has confronted. Oooh, scary! That's patently silly, of course, but it happens all the time. I remember a workshop where we dealt with a story about a monk. He was a misfit in his monastery; the other monks were convinced he had no vocation. At the end of a long story that repeatedly demonstrated his discomfort with monastic life, this misfit monk leaves his cell in the early hours of the morning just as the sun is coming up and he goes to the end of the monastery's property line, crosses just beyond it, and buries something in the snow. End of story. We never know what he buries or why or what this means. The big point, I suppose, is that he crosses the line. But is this a pagan rite of some sort? Is he burying old love letters? Contraceptives? A murder weapon? It could be anything, and as long as we're that free to roam through possibilities, we're unable to experience any genuine emotion, to give the story any real response.

Q: *Do you think the author knew what the monk was hiding?*

JL: I don't think so. I think he was being deliberately mysterious under the delusion that a monk hiding something in the snow would offer the reader a special kind of titillation. I suspect he thought that not knowing made the story richer.

Q: *Even when the story requires that certain things be left out, shouldn't the writer know what is not being revealed?*

JL: Absolutely. A writer has to know a character's age and his motivation and his fate within the story even though none of these is explicitly stated in the story. I can't tell you how often in workshop the question arises, "How old is this child supposed to be?" And the answer cannot be, "Somewhere around ten or twelve." There's a vast difference between ten and twelve and this child is one or the other. He is who he is, he's lived only this long, he has these fears and these hopes. He's a specific person with as much right to his individuality as anybody else in the story. The hard facts of a life leave little room for vagueness. But even where you can legitimately be vague—a character's looks, for instance—I think it's important that the writer himself should know exactly the color of the character's hair and eyes, the shape of his chin, the length of his nose. A writer should know particulars even when he decides not to spell them out.

Hemingway unintentionally propagated a lot of future obscurantists with his iceberg theory: the 1/7th of the iceberg you see lies on top of the 6/7th you can't see, and it's the hidden dimension that gives force and solidity to what is actually visible. Similarly, he said, a story gains force and solidity from the 6/7h the writer knows but does not share with his reader. It's a lovely theory and it catches a truth about the need to know your subject thoroughly. But some people forget Hemingway's point was that the writer has to know what's down there beneath the surface, and it's the known but not expressed element that gives the story its specific gravity.

Q: *Shall we go on to another student? Some time ago we were talking about Isaac Bashevis Singer and you said you taught his niece.*

JL: I should interrupt to say right here that in these interviews I'm bound to leave out people who mattered greatly to me and to the writing program and I apologize right now. If anybody ever reads this and wants a nearly complete record of the people who were in the program—from Edward Abbey to Patricia Zelver—he/she should consult a huge book I edited in 1989 to celebrate the Stanford Centennial. It's called *The Uncommon Touch,* and it's published by the Stanford Alumni Association, and it's always available at the Stanford Bookstore. I gathered stories and poems by 99 of our writers, from the establishment of the program by Wally Stegner in 1947 up to the moment of the Centennial. The book is dedicated to Wally on his eightieth birthday.

Q: *"After this brief commercial . . . "*

JL: Right, back to Brett Singer, an interesting young woman. She came here for an M.A. when we were still offering one and she was writing these little vignettes. They had life and an extraordinary intensity packed into a few pages. She was very smart and, according to her own testimony, she had a lively interest in the drug culture of the 1960s. She got serious very quickly and while she was finishing up her M.A. she began a novel called *The Petting Zoo,* which she completed while she was teaching here. She was a fine critic, an inspiring teacher, and a genuine eccentric. She once came into my office before she taught class and she was wearing an emerald-green satin cocktail dress, split down to her waist, and this was her teaching garb for the day. Simply unbelievable. She was an extraordinary sight in the corridors of a university building and I can't imagine what it was like for those students in her class. She was in her mid to late twenties, very attractive, very smart. I confess I loved her flamboyance and chalked it up to the vagaries of talent. I expected her to become an important writer with a serious career. Perhaps she will yet.

Q: *I'm getting the impression that the writing program was a little more—to use your word—flamboyant than it is today. Am I right?*

JL: They were great days in the writing program actually, the mid-Seventies. Raymond Carver left Stanford just as I arrived. Scott Turow was still teaching here. Bill Kittredge was in my first class, along with Alice Hoffman and Joanne Meschery. And not long afterward we had Toby Wolff and Allan Gurganus, Stephanie Vaughn and Michael Koch, Ron Hansen and Harriet Doerr. They weren't all here at the same time, but they overlapped. Mind you, those weren't the easiest days in the program because we still had the M.A. It was complicated. Do you want me to talk about the writing program as it was then?

Q: *That's why we're here.*

JL: Gosh, it's complicated. There were the Stegner Fellowships that provided a packet of money to three people in fiction, two in poetry, and Fellows simply had to attend workshop and write their own stuff. Being a Fellow was testimony that you were pretty special. In the very same class, sitting around the very same table, there were a bunch of M.A. candidates—the number varied each year— and they had to pay tuition and support themselves. That was bad enough but they were also obliged to take English courses and write term papers in addition to attending workshop and writing fiction. One group got money and took no classes. The others got no money and had heavy class obligations. So there were built-in tensions. What really exacerbated the situation was when an M.A. candidate happened to be a better writer than the Stegner Fellows, and this was embarrassingly demonstrable in M.A. candidates like Scott Turow and Alice Hoffman and Brett Singer. These three made no fuss about it, but I'm sure it must have galled them to see some Fellow who was doing inferior work getting a handsome stipend while they themselves had to pay up and take lit classes and churn out the eternal term paper. Eventually, in the '80s, the tension became palpable, hard words were exchanged and some metaphorical blood was let. I decided something had to be done about the situation. That's when I conceived the idea of letting other universities continue to offer M.A. degrees while we poured all our money into Fellowships. Our M.A. students were terrific in some cases, but for me it was just a question of putting our money where it would do the most good, and that seemed to me to lie with an all-Fellowship program. Needless to say, I had to raise a lot—an awful lot—of money from benefactors to make this possible, and it took years, but I did it. And it's worked out well.

Where were we?

Q: *You were talking about Hansen and Wolff and that group.*

JL: Right. Shall I talk about them individually? So many of them became my close friends.

Q: *Go.*

JL: Ron Hansen's is an interesting story. He was fresh out of Iowa but he had been in the army. It had been his job to go to the families of soldiers who had been killed and tell them what had happened. Hansen was a huge guy with an innocent face and a Huckleberry Finn look to him and I guess the army thought he was the perfect bearer of bad news. He looked like an advertisement for clean living and the promise of eternal life. In any case, by the time he got here he was well embarked on a serious literary book called *Desperadoes.* It was a novel about the Dalton gang, heavily researched and meticulously accurate. Well, he put it up for criticism and got a very disappointing reaction. He was told by somebody in workshop and by Dick Scowcroft who was the director that he should either write it as a shoot-em-up—a yellow-covered thriller from the beginning of the century—or, given the fine writing and the careful research, write it as a factual history of train robberies in general and the Daltons in particular. I thought the novel had every possibility of being a good literary novel set in the old West at the very moment it was turning into the new West, and I encouraged him to go on with it. I didn't have to encourage much because he had drafted the whole thing and was determined to do it. And he did. A really wonderful job. A terrific piece of writing. His gift has always been for colorful writing and sometimes he goes over the top in metaphor and simile—we quarreled, pleasantly, about this—but it was a fine piece of work. Before the year was over he sent it off to his agent, who liked it, and the agent sent it off to Knopf. Ron went off immediately and bought himself an answering machine. This was in the late '70s before everybody in the world owned one. I asked him, "What is that for?" And he told me, "In case the agent or the publisher phones me, I want to be able to get the call even if I'm not home." So I broke the news that it might take weeks to hear from the agent, possibly even months, so he shouldn't be over-anxious. This was on a Wednesday, I think. On Monday morning he came in and said, "I sold my book!" The agent had sent it off to a publisher and simultaneously to a friend, Robert Coover, who wrote *The Universal Baseball Association* and *The Public Burning,* about the Rosenbergs. Coover gave him a sensational blurb and simultaneously the publisher—Knopf—gave him a huge advance, and all this happened over a single weekend. It's a story that's given hope to every young writer I know.

Desperadoes has sold to the movies off and on for years but, like most books bought for the movies, it's never been filmed. Ron followed *Desperadoes* with another novel set in the West, *The Assassination of Jesse James by the Coward Robert Ford.* That book is being filmed right now—lots and lots of movie money for Ron—and I think it's going to star Brad Pitt, so it should get good, close attention. They're two very good literary novels. But I always remember the story as an example of what can go wrong in a workshop: good intentions and bad advice.

Q: *How about Tobias Wolff.*

JL: A very different story. He was here before Ron, actually. Toby was constantly at work, a very prolific guy. He wrote long stories, sometimes too long, and so for him learning to be a successful writer was a question of learning to cut and condense. And he learned it somehow by osmosis; I suppose by seeing how the workshop reacted to his work. I don't recall anyone ever saying to him, "This is what you should do," but from people's reactions he was able to figure out how to make the story an effective piece of work. He's another guy for whom I was less a teacher than a supporter. Much of that first book, *In the Garden of the North American Martyrs,* was written in his year here. But his triumph came with his superb *This Boy's Life.* We had all heard those stories at parties as Toby developed them over the years, first as short anecdotes he told and eventually as terrific set-pieces and then finally, in the writing process, as fine art. It was a fascinating process of transformation.

Toby was then, as he is now, very private about what he writes, and I think that has served him well. Very little outside interference.

Q: *And Harriet Doerr?*

JL: Harriet was born in 1910 so when she came here in the late 1970s she was no chicken. She had left Smith College to marry and in the late '70s, after her husband died, she returned to college to finish her bachelor's degree. I gather she must have transferred her ancient credits from Smith. In her senior year here, aged 69, she peeked into my office and gave me a small sheaf of sketches she had written and immediately ran off. A week later she came back and asked if I had read her stories and if she could be in my summer school class. I told her yes, anybody can; all you have to do is pay the considerable Stanford tuition. She wasn't really writing stories, but I was fascinated that at her great age she wanted to produce fiction, so I bought her lunch (raspberry yoghurt) and we had a good chat and that was the start of our friendship. Later she told me how her husband had inherited an abandoned silver mine in Mexico and how, together, they got the mine going again from absolutely nothing. And how, having raised her two children in Pasadena, she found herself spending what she thought of as her last years in a tiny town in Mexico. It's all in the book, fictionalized of course, but it's there. She didn't tell me until a couple years later that she was the last living Huntington . . . of the railroad Huntingtons, the Huntington Library, etc. She liked to keep that secret, she said, though it was something she was terribly proud of. And why not?

So she was in my summer class in '78, writing these stories--sketches , really, about life in Mexico. But one of them about the stoning of a man called Jose Reyes concluded with a long passage that showed real promise, so I asked her if I could use the manuscript in class to demonstrate how cutting and shaping could make a scene work. She realized that the scene was all over the lot—she suspended the act of stoning the man to ruminate, disastrously, about the nature of stoning and the nature of life and death—but she had no idea why that was a problem. So with her permission I used it as an example of how a scene could be cut and shaped so that it rose up off the paper. I think that was the day she began to think she could become a writer. She was never easy to convince, but gradually she came to see that the hazy impressionism of her prose could be made to accommodate the concrete and the practical and become more effective.

I was so impressed by the way she responded to criticism, and the degree to which her writing improved after it, that I invited her to sit in on my graduate workshop the following year. She did that for two years running. She rented a tiny house on Dartmouth Street and we became close friends; we went to dinner at least three times a week, sometimes more, and we talked endlessly, endlessly about her writing, its great strengths, and the inherent weakness of florid prose that gets out of hand. In her third or fourth year we awarded her a Stegner Fellowship, which made her at last a full, legitimate member of the workshop.

By this time she was writing stories that seemed to have a natural connection and I suggested that she do a series of related stories about two Americans making a new life in Mexico, with their departure and their return as the frame that holds it all together. And she began conceiving the book that way. By the end of the fifth year she had pretty much finished *Stones for Ibarra* as it is today. She would have fiddled around with it forever but I convinced her to let me send it out to a publisher. In the end I tried three different places. I sent it to Billy Abrahams at Holt, Reinhart and Winston who was my own editor at that point. I sent it to Ted Solotaroff at Harper and Row. And I sent it to David Godine at Godine Publishers. They all turned it down. Billy Abrahams said, "It's tragic to turn this down because it's so beautifully written, but it's really from another age. People don't write this way anymore and people don't read this kind of thing anymore." And then I sent it to the Henfield Foundation Contest and she was one of three people who won an award. One of the judges of the contest had a friend at Harcourt, Brace—Cork Smith—and he passed the manuscript on to Cork and that's how the book got published . . . after it had been turned down by three major publishers.

It's interesting too that every story in *Stones for Ibarra* had been rejected by *New Yorker,* but later when the book was published it got this extraordinary rave review by William Maxwell in *New Yorker* itself, and the editor-in-chief began to write her and ask for stories. It was an incredible about-face. Suddenly she had the magic touch. The book was an enormous success. It won a National Book Award especially created for first novels. Harriet became for a while the Eudora Welty of the West Coast. She endowed a Fellowship here with the money from her books. It's in my name, actually. A nice gesture of thanks, don't you think?

Q: *Who else can you tell me about?*

JL: Talking about Harriet and her advanced age brings to mind another older woman I invited to join the workshop as a guest, Mae Briskin. She had published a remarkable book of stories called *A Boy Like Astrid's Mother* that won the PEN West fiction award and she applied with a strong portfolio, but the fact that she had published a book was felt by the committee to put her out of contention for a Fellowship. She lived in Palo Alto, however, so I phoned her up and told her that we loved her work and would she like to sit in on the workshop as a guest. I thought she might be annoyed—she had every right to be—but she accepted the invitation and loved her time here. She began a project that took several years to complete, a novel set in World War II about Christians—some of them priests and nuns—who risked their own lives to help spirit Jews out of Nazi Germany and into France and Italy. This required enormous amounts of research, the study of Italian, and several trips to Italy, where most of the book is set. She produced a wonderful novel called *The Tree Still Stands.* It got raves from the Los Angeles Times and terrific endorsements by Leon Edel and Barbara Kingsolver and was brought out in paperback by Norton. I particularly admire it as a work of enormous intelligence and great generosity of spirit in which the Roman Church comes off perhaps better than it deserves. Subsequently Mae used her familiarity with Italy in a novel—she's now well into her 70s—called *A Hole in the Water,* about a mature woman's search for her lost daughter and the unexpected discovery of her true self after an extra-marital affair. It's a daring piece of work, sexy and mature, and it's very satisfying. Mae never achieved Harriet's celebrity, but she's a great woman and one of my lifelong friends.

Q: *Say more. It's an important program and it's been around a long time.*

JL: Well, there are lots of people. I could go down the list of those 99 writers on the back cover of *The Uncommon Touch,* I suppose. Are we talking just about my friends or about big names from the program or what? I'm not clear about this any more.

Q: *You can use that list on the back of* The Uncommon Touch *if you want or just talk about your friends.*

JL: I'll use the list, but first I should mention Stephanie Vaughn and Michael Koch who are among my closest friends. Stephanie directs the writing program at Cornell now and Michael edits *Epoch* magazine there. Do you know the magazine? It's a really superior quarterly. Stephanie is one of the most talented short story writers I know. She published a terrific book called *Sweet Talk* that got great reviews—much of it had appeared in *New Yorker*—and after that she got deep into a novel, but it has never appeared and she seems not to be publishing anything much these days. Stephanie and Mike were here with Ron Hansen and Harriet and company and we all spent a lot of time together.

Here, let me see the list. Yes, there's Michelle Carter who was my assistant in putting *The Uncommon Touch* together. She wrote a novel called *On Other Days While Going Home* that her publisher said would make her the next generation's Kerouac, something I never quite understood since she wrote so much better than Kerouac, but the novel didn't really catch on the way it should have. She teaches at S. F. State and has become a remarkable playwright. Most recently she wrote *Hillary and Sun-Yi Shop for Ties,* a hilarious send up of women betrayed, and she's been commissioned to write a musical on the life and work of the Unibomber. It's far out stuff and she's wildly talented. I've never met anyone who didn't love Michelle.

Then there's Katharine Andres, whom we've already talked about, and Ivy Goodman, quiet as a mouse and a devastating writer. I always open my course in the Development of the Short Story by reading them a little two page story by Ivy called "Last Minutes." The opening sentences go like this: "I was fifteen on the fifteenth. My father died on the first, my grandmother on the twelfth, my boyfriend on the eighteenth. 'You're next,' my mother said to me on the twenty-second. She handed me a pack of razor blades and a blue revolver. 'Do me a favor,' she said, 'and for God's sake, don't make a mess.'" It's a stunning opening and the rest of the little story lives up to it, a study in teen alienation and despair. I loved Ivy.

Allan Gurganus, we've talked about him. Alice Hoffman. Deborah Larsen, a remarkable poet, who lately has turned to fiction and published a superb novel called *The White,* based on the true story of an 18th century white girl who was kidnapped by Iroquois, raised among them, and who, when rescued, chose to stay among them. It's a fascinating story and it's superbly crafted. Ralph Lombreglia, *Men Under Water.* Let me see, I'm skipping around now. There's

Erin McGraw, a wonderful story writer and novelist who wrote *The Baby Tree, Lies of the Saints, The Seamstress of Hollywood Boulevard.* A fine writer and a generous, thoughtful person. She married Andrew Hudgins, the poet, who was a Fellow in poetry at the same time she was a Fellow in fiction. A great match. Tom McNeal, *Goodnight, Nebraska,* an old, solid, devoted friend. Dennis McFarland, a superb writer whose first book, *The Music Room,* was reviewed on the front page of the *New York Times Book Review* and who should be famous by now. I don't know why he's not. I'm skipping again. Here's Vikram Seth, who was a poet here, but went on to write *A Suitable Boy,* an international best seller, even bigger in England than here.

And Brent Spencer. Brent is an extraordinary writer. He's written a book of stories called *Are We Not Men?* It's one of the best collections I've read in years and years, but it's never been brought out in paperback so it's not as known as it should be. Each story is a world unto itself, it's about something that matters, and it's written by a consummate craftsman. I've taught his work several times in my story class. His novel *The Lost Son* is in part autobiographical and it's a hair-raiser about the effects a brutal father has on his only child. It makes for a searing read. Brent teaches at Creighton University and runs the writing program there. I'm crazy about his work.

Q: *Is that his background? Midwest.*

JL: Yes, he's a farmer. He's a farmer who went and got a Ph.D. in poetry at Penn State and somehow drifted into writing fiction. He came to us from Iowa, as so many writers do, and he taught undergraduates here for three years. When he left Stanford, he went to teach at Creighton, fell in love with Nebraska, and has remained there ever since. He is married to Jonis Agee—James Agee's niece—who wrote *The River Wife,* and they live on a farm and write.

That's a quick look at the list, I guess.

Q: *What about people who aren't on the list?*

JL: You mean people who came here after *The Uncommon Touch* was published? There are so many really good writers among them. I'm thinking of Fenton Johnson and David Vann and Jason Brown and Keith Scribner and Samantha Chang and Bo Caldwell and Peter Rock and Ryan Harty and Julie Orringer and Z.Z. Packer. Let me see. Tom Barbash, Katharine Noel, Eric Puchner, Adam Johnson, Angela Pneumann, Stephen Elliott and the two Toms: Tom Kealey and Tom McNealy. These are all people who have written books, good ones, and there are several more with books that are going to be important, I know. Sharon May and Josh Tyree stand out in particular. And Harriet Clark.

Q: *So that's it on students. Surely there must be some startling stories about these people whose names you've just run through. We've got more time. Give it some thought.*

JL: I'll tell you two stories, one about Fenton Johnson and one about David Vann. They were both Stanford undergraduates when I first taught them and then years later they returned to Stanford as Fellows, so I knew them particularly well. Both of these stories illustrate something about the insane nature of the writing profession.

Fenton teaches writing at the University of Arizona and he has just published a fascinating book on problems of belief and disbelief called *Keeping Faith: A Sceptic's View,* nonfiction, of course. But when he was here he was engaged solely with fiction. The moment I'm recalling is when he wrote a short story about a city guy's encounter with a gay cowboy, sort of surreal and touching and funny, but it never worked as well as he wanted it to, so he kept on rewriting it and each time he'd bring me the new version. Well, we reached a point when I had critiqued the twelfth version—truly, the twelfth—only to have him show up with a thirteenth. I said, to him. "I don't know, Fenton. I don't have any idea which version I'm looking at here. I've seen so many drafts that they're all superimposed on one another in my mind. My suggestion is to get rid of it. Send it out for publication and see what happens." He sent it out and it was published immediately. But I'm convinced that if he hadn't sent it out, he'd have done twenty more versions and we both would have found something wrong with each of them. The point of this anecdote, I guess, is knowing when to let go. "A short story is never really finished; it's only abandoned." Somebody said that, or should have.

The David Vann story is rather more lively. He is a really gifted guy whose childhood was marked—not ruined, though nearly—by his father's suicide at age forty. David, who was still just a kid, was the one who found the body. David writes about this again and again; indeed, he's just won the Grace Paley award for his novel, *Legend of a Suicide.* It's not surprising that he expects life to be brief and nasty, though his sunny attitude toward everything would make you think he's never had a care.

As I've said, he was a Stanford undergraduate, and after graduation he did an MFA at Cornell, where he also taught for a year or two, and then he got a Fellowship here. He published a terrific story called "Ichthyology" in *Atlantic* about the loneliness and horror of a child who is—almost accidentally—abandoned. Well, he got a teaching job here, and he expanded it into a Continuing Studies job, and the next thing I knew he was teaching writing seminars on board a small ship he had bought—the "Grendel"—and these seminars were a roaring success. He bought the ship with a huge bank loan and captained it himself; he had grown up on ships in Alaska and he had all the necessary permits and licenses and so forth. He was breaking even on the deal, perhaps even making a profit, by the time his contract with Stanford came to an end. I asked him then if he had found another teaching job and he assured me he had a better plan, one that would give him much more free time to write. "Tell Uncle," I said—we were fast friends by this time—and with a knowing grin he told me that he was having a ship built, in Turkey no less, and he would run writing seminars on the Mediterranean for half the year and write for the other half. Some prosperous fans of his writing seminars had offered to loan him money to buy the ship, a first-class deal, and it would cost only a few hundred thousand dollars. "I'm buying myself time to write," he said, as if this would convince me. I listened in disbelief and lowered my forehead to the desk for a minute while he laughed nervously, and then he stopped laughing and said, "Are you all right?" I looked up at him—he was gleaming with hope—and I said something like, "You're buying time to write? Well, I can see what will happen. You'll make some money, you'll buy a bigger ship, the ship will sink, you'll write a best seller about the sinking, and with your royalties you'll have much more free time to write. I foresee a happy ending." He laughed and I laughed and that's more or less how it unfolded . . . although in an infinitely more complicated series of events. The actual sinking involved a "perfect storm," Mediterranean pirates—yes, they still exist—blind heroism, near drowning, and a German rescue ship whose captain let David's ship sink so that he could claim it as salvage. The book is called *A Mile Down: The True Story of a Disastrous Career at Sea.* It's a thriller, beautifully written, artfully crafted, a really fascinating book. David's a great kid.

Q: *Where is Vann now? Did it buy him time to write?*

JL: (Laughs.) David still sails—at this moment, in fact, he's sailing around the world on a commission from *Esquire* to write about the trip—but he's married now and he has settled down to teach at University of San Francisco and—since some things sometimes turn out right—he has plenty of time to write.

Q: *This is a good place to stop.*

JL: With David still afloat. And writing.

INTERVIEW 6

Q: *Looking back over our previous interview, I get the impression that you like everyone.*

JL: I like my students. It's the human race I hate.

Q: *(Laughs.) Okay, let's go on to other writers—non-Stanford writers—ones who have influenced you as a writer.*

JL: Good. I've actually given some thought to this over the years and I'm convinced that there are good influences and bad ones; dangerous ones, I should say. For instance, if you write poetry, you don't want to be deeply influenced by T. S. Eliot or Hopkins because they're so powerful and so idiosyncratic that it's almost impossible not to become a second-class imitation of the original. They're glorious but they're dangerous mentors. It's like wanting to write fiction and becoming indentured to James Joyce. It's fatal.

Q: *Who is influential but not fatal? For you, I mean.*

JL: For me that would be Graham Greene and Flannery O'Connor. They both offer a nice clean prose in service of characters and story. That is, in characters who are caught up in life-altering situations that reverberate with the reader at a deep level of feeling and experience. As a writer, that's what I care about: moments that test a character's integrity and tap into our own deepest fears and desires. Greene does that and so does O'Connor.

For satire I have lifted everything I know about timing and outrage from Evelyn Waugh and Muriel Spark. When that Lord Leebrick Theatre Company wrote to say that my play's "treatment of the subject matter verges on the barbarous," they pleased me more than I can tell you. Satire should verge on the barbarous. Waugh's satire always does—take a look at *Vile Bodies,* for instance—and Spark's does as well, though her interest is chiefly moral outrage. She's a more economical writer than Waugh but she's as brilliant and polished a stylist as the great man himself. In fact their polish as writers is precisely what makes their satire seem so monstrous.

Q: *What about contemporary writers?*

JL: Well, I think of Greene and O'Connor and Waugh and Spark as my contemporaries. All of them were alive and writing when I was beginning to write. I think of them as my mentors, true, but as contemporaries as well.

Q: *What about your actual contemporaries like . . .*

JL: Cheever and Updike and Roth? And Paley and Bellow and Malamud? You know, it's funny that all these guys have been to Stanford for the Lane Lecture Series so I've met them all, with varying degrees of admiration. Actually, Updike hasn't been to Stanford. I met him when I worked for Atlantic.

Q: *You mention varying degrees of admiration. I sense a little disappointment in your reaction. Who was disappointing? And how?*

JL: Roth came with his then wife, Claire Bloom, and he was less than—how shall I say—attentive to her, but I shouldn't criticize a guest. They were all fine writers and readers and speakers and that's why we invited them for the Lane Lectures.

Q: *That's your series, isn't it? You started it?*

JL: It was my idea. But it was Bill Lane who funded it, handsomely, and then endowed it in perpetuity. Glorious friends of the writing program, Jean and Bill Lane.

Q: *That lecture series has brought a lot of famous writers to Stanford, some more famous than others and some who will last longer than others. Everybody agrees on Hemingway, Fitzgerald, and Faulkner as the great writers of the first half of the twentieth century, isn't that right? Who do you think will be their counterparts in the second half?*

JL: God knows. It may well be the ones we've mentioned: Cheever and Updike, Bellow and Roth. It's hard to guess what this new century will want to read . . . if indeed they want to read at all. But Updike's Rabbit novels have staying power and Cheever's stories—think of "The Country Husband" or "The Swimmer"—are surely going to live. Bellow's novels, all of them, are models of intelligence and insight and much more than that. He's an acute observer and a sharp critic of the culture he writes about—he captures it flawlessly—and his Augie March and Moses Herzog and Arthur Sammler are characters that have staying power for at least the next century. Roth is a different kind of writer; he's caught the sexual obsession and maniacal concentration on self that seems to characterize the final quarter of the twentieth century. So I suppose these guys will go on being read. It's an interesting problem, isn't it.

Q: *Who else would you like to see being read in the future?*

JL: Among Americans, you mean? Grace Paley. Joyce Oates, McCarthy's *The Road,* DeLillo's *Underworld,* Richard Powers' *The Echo Maker.*

I love Grace Paley. She's a very quirky writer with a relatively small body of work. When I was a staff editor at *Atlantic* two of her tiny stories, "Wants" and "Needs" came across my desk and I was entranced by them. I wrote on the memo sheet that accompanied all submissions, "This woman seems to be a New York housewife who hasn't a clue about conventional story-telling but these are captivating little stories and I recommend we take them." She had already published a book and I should have known who she was, of course. I told her this anecdote when she visited here and she was delighted. "It's good to be famous," she said. She was one of the warmest, most down to earth writers I've ever met.

Q: *What do you mean by quirky?*

JL: The forms her stories take are unlike anything we're familiar with: little reminiscences, anecdotes with a moral tag attached, a style that verges from the vernacular to the divine within a single sentence. A few of her stories are quite long. She has no fixed idea of what a story should look like. She's concerned only with what it does to you.

Q: *Yes?*

JL: Take, for instance, her great story "Friends." It's about three middle-aged women, housewives by trade, who go to visit a fourth who is dying of cancer. Instead of telling the story straight-on in a third person narrative—this is who they are and this is what they did—she tells the story from the point of view of a character who has her own peculiar obsessions and worries, so that everything you perceive about what these characters say and do has to be reexamined with her lopsided perceptions in mind. So you get the story twice, once with the facts as reported and a second time when you straighten out those facts for yourself. Paley does this all the time. She's not unique in this, of course, but it's not a matter of the typical unreliable narrator, either. It's more complicated than that. Shall I go on, or is this already lethal?

Q: *I'm interested.*

JL: Well, here's the story: three friends visit a dying friend. The first thing you notice is that the narrative is not causal but sequential, and the narrator constantly interrupts herself to qualify what she says and to identify feelings and explicate relationships. She's a narrator who's less interested in self-examination than in self-effacement; she's part of the group but slightly removed from it, and this allows her that independent commentary we're forced to examine. She gives us a section devoted to each woman as she is in herself, with her family, her hopes, her heartbreaks, so that in the end the story is less a memory than a commemoration, a kind of memorial service for the dead. She fixes these people on paper as they were and as they are. Forever. It's subtle and complicated, with major and minor disappointments played off against one another within a single sentence. I always remember this great sentence about two of the women: "They were in furious discussion; they were holding hands." It characterizes in just a few words both the ferocity of their independence and their loyalty to each other.

Q: *I should read Paley.*

JL: Everybody should read Paley. She came here for the Lane Lecture Series and she was an enormous hit. She's a great reader; the quirkiness seems inevitably right when she reads her own work.

Q: *Would you say Flannery O'Connor is quirky?*

JL: I'd say she was difficult. Straight out difficult because reading her with any understanding requires a knowledge of the Judeo-Christian tradition as well as the willingness to suspend disbelief and to accept for the time being her brand of Catholicism, which in fact is pretty Jansenistic. She presumes as a given that God exists and that he interferes in our lives with a purpose, and she expects her readers to believe that too. Or at least to suspend disbelief. Of course Dante and Milton and Eliot make similar demands—they assume you accept the Judeo-Christian architecture of creation, heaven, and hell—but somehow those demands seem easier to meet when you're talking about Dante and Milton and Eliot. O'Connor doesn't pack their wallop, but she is indeed a fine writer. To my thinking she's the finest short story writer of the twentieth century. I want to say, parenthetically, that Chekhov died in 1904 and nobody's stories are better than Chekhov's. Given her subject matter, or at least the religious aspects of it, I find it amazing that she's popular, at all. She's been extremely fortunate in her critics and explicators; without them—Allen Tate and Sally Fitzgerald and Kathleen Feeley—she might never have made it into the canon that includes Hemingway and Cheever and Carver, especially when you consider that her body of work is relatively small. It's a lot larger than Paley's but small nonetheless. O'Connor has been lucky. As well as good.

Q: *What do you think of the proposition that sometimes a writer's value lies in the quantity of work that he's produced?*

JL: Like, say . . . ?

Q: *Balzac. Or perhaps even Dostoyevsky.*

JL: Balzac certainly. Or Joyce Oates in our own time.

Q: *Could it be that if you leave a vast body of work behind, you can't be ignored? That the sheer quantity means it cannot be left unexamined?*

JL: Quality has to come in for consideration somewhere along the line. We're not talking about Dickens or Trollope, I take it, men who are important writers in themselves. Or are we?

Q: *We're talking about prolific writers. You can choose anyone you want.*

JL: Well, that stops me in my tracks. Let me see. If we exclude Dickens and Trollope there are certainly prolific writers whom nobody reads from the nineteenth and twentieth centuries. Winston Churchill, for instance. Not the great British politician of World War II but the American novelist. He was so famous that when the British Churchill visited the States on lecture tours, he began using his middle name, Spencer, to differentiate himself from the novelist. In the early 1900s the American Churchill was on the top of the Best Seller list year after year and he had this huge body of work that, apparently, sold like crazy. Nobody reads him today. I don't know anybody who has even heard of him, let alone read him. On a more exalted plane there's Howells and Sinclair Lewis and the guy who wrote *Studs Lonigan.*

Q: *James Farrell.*

JL: James T. Farrell, right. Farrell had a vast body of work, larger even than Norman Mailer's because he went on writing for thirty or forty years after *Lonigan* and, though much of his stuff has been published, it's been largely ignored. I've read somewhere that he has a huge pile of unpublished manuscripts just sitting in a safe somewhere in Chicago. So I don't think a large body of work is enough to guarantee you'll be taken seriously by a future generation or, in Farrell's case, by the present one. On the other hand, I think your suggestion that volume counts may apply to Trollope, whose novels were important in his lifetime but never ranked up there with Dickens or Tolstoy, though he's still read today. The body of his work cannot be ignored because it contains a few novels that people keep going back to. My friend Nancy Packer, an excellent writer and critic herself, maintains that he's equal to if not better than Dickens. And she's one smart reader. I guess the conclusion is that it's better to have a large body of work than not.

Q: *Was the American Winston Churchill treated seriously during his lifetime? The way, for instance, Norman Mailer is?*

JL: I don't really know that. He was taken seriously by the Best Seller List, but that doesn't count.

Q: *Maybe you disagree that people take Norman Mailer seriously.*

JL: Oh, I think they do. I think even beyond popular culture, even deep in the clannish thickets of the *New York Review of Books,* he's taken seriously. And he'll survive, I think, because he's written books that have won major awards, and once you've got major awards your work is going to be looked at in the future. If there's stuff worth saving, it will be saved; that's where quality comes in. Mailer has written *The Naked and the Dead,* which I've never been able to get through, and *The Executioner's Song,* which is brilliant, and those political books about the march on Washington and so forth. I can't imagine that his novels, particularly the late ones, will be taken very seriously, but *The Naked and the Dead* will remain an important Second World War document.

Q: *Document?*

JL: I don't mean it as a put-down.

Q: *Can't we give him some points for trying very hard to be honest?*

JL: I'm willing to give him lots of points but I don't give anybody points for trying to be honest. Honesty, like sincerity, is subjective; it's about the author's feelings and intentions; it can be fatal to literature. It gets in the way of the pursuit of hard, objective truth. And truth, by its nature, is mysterious.

Q: *But that's exactly what I mean by honest; I think he pursues hard objective truth.*

JL: Then I'll give him points . . . on your behalf. I thought you were talking about sincerity, which is a real problem in writing. Sincerity is a half-shade off of outright sentimentality and that way lies the death of real emotion. I'm hopped up on the question of sincerity and sentimentality because it's always been a problem among undergrad writers. You have to fight it.

Have you read *Crime and Punishment* lately? I'm rereading it now after some thirty or forty years, so it's new to me except for the principal events which, of course, stay with you. But the writing—no matter what translation you read—is very rough and repetitive. It's a kind of slow-motion novel, there are endless pages of interior monologue, lots of recapitulation, lots of what seem to me stylistic crudities, but then there's a moment of such horrendous truth that you realize Dostoyevsky's sincerity or lack of it could have nothing to do with it. That moment comes right after Raskolnikov has finished his rehearsal for the murder of the old lady. He falls asleep and has this terrible, terrible dream of a peasant who is inviting all his friends and even strangers to get up on his wagon so he can give them a ride. And his wagon is to be pulled by an old, dying mare. Of course there's no way the mare can pull the wagon when it's empty, let alone with people in it, and the peasant keeps putting on more and more people and whipping the mare and he calls on other people to help him whip the mare. "Keep whipping her. Keep whipping her," he's shouting, until finally the only thing the mare can do is sink on its back heels and collapse to the ground where they beat it to death with wooden staves.

It's the most relentless presentation I've ever read of humans indulging in cruelty simply because they can. And the effect has nothing to do with Dostoyevsky's sincerity or his honesty or his feeling for the horse. It has to do with his ability to create a moment in which we perceive how low we can stoop, how small and hideous we can be, especially when we're cheered on in our blood lust by other people. As if, with the collusion of others, our own bestiality can find lower depths, and lower still. That scene works unforgettably because Dostoyevsky creates a revelation of the human race at its very worst. His sincerity has nothing to do with its effectiveness.

If you want to see how sincerity can falsify feeling and destroy a scene, take a look at the film of "Schindler's List." You've seen it, the Holocaust movie. Toward the end there's that unnecessary and disastrous moment that undercuts everything we've learned about Oscar Schindler when he tears off his wristwatch and says something like, "Damn this wrist watch! It could have saved ten more people! Why didn't I give this?" and he goes on and on until he moves himself to tears. It's a speech that's utterly sincere and it's straight from the heart of Steven Spielberg. But it's not true to Schindler's character. Sometimes you have to sacrifice your deepest feelings for the good of the story. Mind you, Spielberg is a genius, despite this little lapse.

Q: *What about Gore Vidal? I know you like his essays.*

JL: His novels don't seem to me very important. His essays, though, are always very smart, very funny, very bitchy, whether he's writing about literature or politics or his disappointment with the way humanity has let him down. He's a very canny literary critic and he deplores the level of criticism you find in book reviews today. "Book chat," he calls it. His own criticism always reveals something new and illuminating about the writer, as when he deals with Calvino or Nabokov or "The Hacks of Academe," as he calls literature professors who dare to write about fiction. Lately, in his dotage, he's been writing stuff that depends for its effect on his personality rather than on his mind.

Q: *Have you had a chance yet to look at Myers' booklet?*

JL: I did and I have it right here. He's one fierce dude, is Myers.

Q: *Well, what did you think? Does he make sense to you?*

JL: He makes a lot of sense. I love the title, *A Reader's Manifesto: An Attack on the Growing Pretentiousness in American Literary Prose.* And I like the way he singles out literary prose, as if he might well have included editorial writers and sports columnists and political pundits, even though for the moment he's decided to give them a reprieve. I recall a commentator at the last Olympics saying, "Just check the historicity of the sport." And Tony Soprano's sister Janet demanding the return of some old records, "I want that discography returned immediately." And a sports announcer the other day saying, "I'm just guessing, probabilistically." Apparently the whole world wants to talk pretty and sound deep. No wonder Myers felt obliged to restrict himself to literature.

Q: *He's a linguist, you know.*

JL: Well, he's very smart and I'm proud that *Atlantic* published this in the original version because it's very daring. Myers takes on some big names and you know that they and their friends are going to barbecue him if he ever tries to publish fiction himself. I mean, he tells that unthinkable story about Oprah phoning Toni Morrison to say that she had been forced to puzzle repeatedly over some sentences in

Beloved and Morrison responds: "That, my dear, is called reading." The grandeur and the self-importance in that reply take your breath away.

Myers is very smart and he knows how to read. He's arguing in terms of what he thinks is pure logic, but in fact it's logic that is conditioned by a distinct prejudice for the kind of prose he likes: simple, clear, and forceful. Windowpane prose. It's prose I like as well, and so do you, because it suppresses all distractions and invites the reader straight into the story where reactions are elicited for a particular emotional or psychological payoff. Myers' victims, the New Pretenders, want to show off a little bit and write pretty language—it's fun, after all—but I confess I agree with him on almost every passage he condemns. The sex scene in Guterson's *Snow Falling on Cedars,* for instance, is a howl. It's simply awful and I'm quite right in saying that if Jackie Collins had written that, the critics would have had a field day. However—and this is a terrible admission—I read that book and I have no recollection of that passage. I must have just read through it and kept on going. Apparently you get a certain momentum when you're reading a book whose story or characters you're involved with and you forgive a lot of stuff that's really bad.

Q: *Or maybe you just don't want to see the flaws.*

JL: Because you're working with the author? Maybe. But I should have . . . if I had read that sex scene with even the slightest attention to language, I'd have stopped immediately, or at least I'd have taken my pen and put an exclamation point in the margin.

Q: *Read what he says about the sex scene.*

JL: Well, I'll read a little of it. Myers writes, "Guterson knows that he has no gift for figurative language. As a result he sinks below mediocrity as rarely as he rises above it." Ouch! "Only the sex scenes are laughably bad." And then he quotes the scene. Shall I read it? Can you stand it?

> The head of his penis found the place it wanted. For a moment he waited there, poised, and kissed her . . . Then with his hands he pulled her to him and at the same time entered her so that she felt his scrotum slap against her skin. Her entire body felt the rightness of it, her entire body was seized to it. Hatsue arched her shoulder blades—her breasts pressed themselves against his chest—and a slow shudder ran through her.
>
> "It's right," she remembered whispering. "It feels so right, Kaabuo."
>
> "Tadaima aware ga wakatta," he had answered. "I understand just now the deepest beauty."

Myers points out the essential silliness of the searching penis, the shudder's slow run, and of course that scrotum slap heard round the world. And then he goes after the Japanese translation. "What Kabuo is saying here," Myers says, is 'Now I understand pity,' a mood killer if ever there was one." He's a funny guy and he knows how to isolate bad prose so that it stands out in all its badness.

He does the same thing with the ineptitude of Paul Auster's imagery. Let me read you a passage about the dog, Mr. Bones: "His nostrils were turned into suction tubes . . . " The image it conjures up is ludicrous. "His nostrils were turned into suction tubes, snuffing up scents in the way a vacuum cleaner inhales bits of glass. And there were times, many times in fact, when Willie marveled at the fact that the sidewalk did not crack apart from the force and fury of Mr. Bones' snout work." Myers goes on quoting Auster on the vacuum cleaner nose and the dog's refusal to move on "before he had ingested the full savor of the turd or urine puddle under his scrutiny. So unbudgeable did he become, so firmly did he anchor himself to the spot, that Willie wondered if there wasn't a sac somewhere hidden in his paws that could secrete glue on command." Myers dismantles this passage to show how unfortunate the comparison is—a nose and a vacuum cleaner—and he demonstrates how an image you conjure up in the reader's mind can become merely laughable and turn against you and your intentions. Guterson's scrotum slapping is the perfect example.

Myers is very good about pointing out how it's the story itself that gets you through these bad passages.

Q: *I'm going to tell you something to get your reaction. When I drove to work from Berkeley, I used to listen to books on tape. When I came home, sometimes I'd go over certain passages in the printed book because I felt I had to see in print what I had heard.*

JL: You wanted more than a merely auditory experience.

Q: *I wanted to see the words on the page. Especially if I had liked the book.*

JL: Which is good.

Q: *But not always helpful. I had a problem with a particular book by one of the authors Myers talks about: Cormac McCarthy for* All The Pretty Horses. *When the book first came out, after reading the* New York Times *review, I decided to read the novel. He was treated very seriously as a major writer.*

JL: Oh, he is. He's thought to be a major stylist.

Q: *But I couldn't read it. When I started listening to the tape, everything just flowed past me. The book is minimally punctuated, if you recall.*

JL: I've never read it. I started it and gave up right away. Maybe we're reading him too closely though. Maybe you have to approach McCarthy's prose the way we approach a collage; you know, not focusing on the individual elements themselves but on their relationship to each other. It's one of those odd things that a collage, when you view it at a distance, will take on a clarity and profundity that it simply can't produce when you view it up close.

Or maybe we should hear Cormac McCarthy read rather than read Cormac McCarthy ourselves. Language should communicate, and if what he wants to communicate is an impression—the way words sound side by side or the connotations they suggest—then maybe that's a valid approach to writing, even though it isn't one I want to pursue. For myself anyway.

Look, I just found the chapter on McCarthy in Myers' book. It's called—a wonderful title—"Muscular Prose." I taught his wife, you know, in the graduate program years and years ago. Lee McCarthy, his first wife. A very interesting woman. She had talent of her own and not long ago she sent me a book of poems she had written—fascinating, visceral stuff—that tells a lot about her as a woman and a writer. It's called *Good Girl* and it's a furious, intelligent, emotionally exhausting book of poems. I loved it.

Here's the passage I was looking for. It's a quote from *Blood Meridian.* "They caught up and set out each day in the dark before the day yet was, and they ate cold meat and biscuit and made no fire." *Before the day yet was. And made no fire.* Very grand stuff, and a little self-important as well.

And here are some cowboys with a hangover:

> "They walked off in separate directions through the chaparral to stand spraddle-legged clutching their knees and vomiting. The browsing horses jerked their heads up. It was no sound they'd ever heard before. In the gray twilight those retchings seemed to echo like the calls of some rude provisional species loosed upon that waste. Something imperfect and malformed lodged in the heart of being. A thing smirking deep in the eyes of grace itself like a gorgon in an autumn pool."

We're talking about men throwing up here, and vomit has rarely taken on such metaphysical importance. The prose has gone mad, with a fake epic quality and a mind-glazing self-importance. It reminds me of Stephen Leacock's satire on Milton. After Adam and Eve ate the apple, Leacock writes, "They brushed their dentures elephantine." I wish I could remember the rest because it's written in that same overblown rhetoric.

Q: *He's got a passage there about the insides of a horse and it's filled with that same kind of metaphysical importance.*

JL: Right. "While inside the vaulting of the ribs between his knees, the darkly-meated heart pumped of who's will and the blood pulsed and the bowels shifted in their massive blue convolutions of who's will and the stout thighbones and knee and cannon and the tendons like flaxen hawsers that drew and flexed and drew and flexed at their articulations of who's will . . . " and on and on. Myers is very canny. He says, "The obscurity of who's will, which has an unfortunate Dr. Seusssian ring to it, is meant to bully readers into thinking that the author's mind operates on a plane higher than their own—a plane where it isn't ridiculous to eulogize the shifts in a horse's bowels." Talk about reductio ad absurdum! I wonder if McCarthy read it and cleaned up his act. There's nothing remotely so self-indulgent as this in *No Country for Old Men* or in *The Road.*

Q: *You like those books?*

JL: They're fascinating. I couldn't put them down, either of them. I think *No Country* may be guilty of exploiting the mindless violence it condemns in its final pages but it certainly is a page turner, and as a testimony to the hideous cruelty humankind is capable of, it's hard to beat. *The Road* is horrifying—it takes place after some unidentified world disaster—and, amid this stupefying wasteland, the story explores the instinct for love and survival between a man and his young son. I found it very moving and, in a way I didn't want to contemplate, very believable. And there's none of that quasi-mystical prose to get in the way of the story. It's a very, very good book. I could die happy if I'd written it.

Q: *Back to Myers for a moment. I think each of these writers has been called—and certainly regards himself—as a stylist. They work at their style. What do you have to say about Annie Proulx?*

JL: I'm afraid I found *The Shipping News* too difficult to get through. I tried. All those little staccato sentences and her penchant for leaving out 'a' and 'the' and then those dazzling images, and I call them dazzling because sometimes your eyes cross just trying to figure them out. Myers quotes a couple. There are better ones, funnier, but these have the merit of being shorter. "Furious dabs of tulips stuttering in gardens." "An apron of sound lapped out of each dive." Since when do dabs stutter? How exactly does an apron lap, except by the invocation of yet another metaphor? I'm afraid I may have given up on her too easily. She wrote the original story of the "Brokeback Mountain" film, I understand, so she must be a really good storyteller. But I can't get past the prose.

Q: *Ultimately, it seems like good writing comes down to the question of honesty.*

JL: Well, straightforwardness perhaps rather than honesty, but of course you and I would conclude to that because of our prejudice. We share this strange notion that the writer should be as invisible as possible and that the story itself is what matters. And we tell ourselves that these writers that Myers takes apart share an even stranger notion that it's the job of the writer to be smarter than the reader and to let him know it . . . by his clever prose, his bright similes and metaphors, and his deep reflections on being and nothingness and the nature of evil. But we have to remember that Proulx and Company take enormous care to produce this kind of prose. She loves her stories and she loves writing them and she feels—I'm certain of it—that she's chosen the perfect language for what she's trying to do.

Let me say something I should have said a moment ago when we were talking about stylists. I have nothing against the lush style in itself. Saintsbury has written at length about the 'Triumph of the Ornate Style,' as he calls it, and it's one of the great glories of English prose. That miraculous rush of poetry you find in Shakespeare has its parallel in the prose of Donne and Milton and Taylor and the authors of the King James Bible, and in my favorite, Sir Thomas Browne. These writers play language as if it's some rare musical instrument and the result is a rhetoric of such lushness that it's ravishing. And I love that stuff. It's suited perfectly to sermons and essays and the Bible, but it simply doesn't lend itself to contemporary fiction. Fictional prose needs to be in service of its narrative. Or so I believe.

Herewith, the end of my rant on style.

Q: *Very good. And what do you think of DeLillo?*

JL: I admire him greatly. I think he's uneven from book to book—I had to fight my way through *The Names* and gave up forty pages from the end—but I loved *Great Jones Street* and *White Noise* and *Libra* and *Underworld*. Until I read *Underworld*, *Libra* was my favorite. It's a speculative study about the character of Lee Harvey Oswald and his assassination of Kennedy. I think that in many ways it's profound. And convincing. It does for Oswald what Joyce Oates' *Blonde* does for Marilyn Monroe: it makes you see a very different and more human character than the one you thought you knew and it elicits sympathy and understanding for how he or she got this way. It's not a triumph of psychology so much as a triumph of art.

Q: *So you didn't find Myers' convincing on DeLillo?*

JL: I confess I like DeLillo so much that I wasn't impressed by Myers' attack on *White Noise* as an attempt by the author "to simply assert what he can't make us feel." The passage he quotes is tedious and repetitive but it's not off-putting in the way I find Annie Proulx to be. I think *White Noise* is a good academic satire and a nice rendering of a screwed-up professor who teaches Hitler Studies. Just the idea of Hitler Studies is terrific, I think. I enjoyed the book.

Q: *And you really liked* Underworld*?*

JL: As a picture of ordinary life in the last half of the twentieth century, I think it's hard to beat. It's about—significantly, in the context—a guy in waste management. His wife is having an affair with one of his friends, and as background to his feckless and pitiful life we have the Cuban missile crisis, the assassinations of Kennedy and King, homelessness, poverty, greed, and the threat of nuclear disaster. It's a catalog of what America has brought on itself in the last fifty years. Incredibly, on the cover of the paperback—published long before 9/11—is a photograph of the twin towers of the World Trade Center and an airplane headed eerily straight at them. It's like an uncanny and unwelcome prophecy.

Q: *So you read him before bed at night?*

JL: What do you mean?

Q: *You said once that you always read for an hour before bed, no matter how late it is.*

JL: Oh, yes. That's true. Sometimes I read fiction but mostly I tend to read history or biography before bed, especially if during the day I'm writing fiction. I have to unwind and I prefer something absolutely irrelevant to what I'm working on.

Q: *So what are you reading now?*

JL: I've just finished Daniel Burnham's *Death in the White City,* which is an account of the 1893 World's Fair in Chicago and how it got put together. Apparently after the Paris World Fair there was the feeling in the U.S. that the Chicago World Fair had to be bigger and better, with something that would challenge the Eiffel Tower for magnificence and folly. So all the major American architects were involved, including Olmsted, who designed our courtyard here at Stanford, not to mention Central Park in New York.

Anyhow, Burnham combines the story of creating the Chicago World's Fair with the story—altogether factual, I believe—of America's first serial killer and how he did in his victims and what a charmer he was. He constructed a big building that would serve temporarily as a hotel and he accepted only women guests, whom he quite literally charmed to death. He had constructed a huge cellar with a furnace in the middle and he would lure his victims down to a small private room where he would gas them to death. He would listen on the other side of the door until they stopped screaming and he could incinerate them in that specially built furnace. Your typical serial killer, I suppose, or at least the first in a long line.

Burnham writes a nice readable prose and he combines these two very different stories in the same book, alternating chapters so that you get the building of the Fair and the building of the hotel for women, and then the success of the Fair and the successful capture of the killer. It's really quite interesting and it has a lot of nice illustrations. That's as close as I get to reading detective fiction.

Q: *But you don't use that time to research the fiction you're working on?*

JL: Well, I'm always doing remote preparation for my Italian book, the one set in Donatello's bottega and sometimes I do that at night before bed. *Brunelleschi's Dome* by Ross King, a popular book—semi-scholarly, I suppose—about how Brunelleschi solved the impossible problem of constructing the dome for the Cathedral in Florence, the Duomo. And Christopher Hibbert's terrific book on the Medicis, *The Rise and Fall of the House of Medici.* And Brucker's *Renaissance Florence.* And the kind of thing I would love to have written if I'd been a scholar, Iris Origo's *The Merchant of Prato.* It's a truly great book, scholarly and easy to read, and it gives you a sense of how ordinary life was lived in fifteenth century Italy.

Q: *Why not write a scholarly book on Donatello?*

JL: Oh, I couldn't. It would take a lifetime of research and my life is practically over. Nor, frankly, do I have the necessary smarts.

Q: *Since you've just mentioned it, let's talk about detective fiction.*

JL: Oh, I thought we were all done.

Q: *One more minute*

JL: Okay. I've tried Dibdin whose detective novels my wife loves; also Donna Leon's. They're set in Venice so I thought the place alone might make it possible for me to read them. But I can never get beyond the first chapter because by the time I hit page ten it always strikes me that I could be reading something equally diverting and a lot more substantial. Jane Austen, for instance.

Q: *You're missing out on some good entertainment.*

JL: So everybody tells me.

INTERVIEW 7

Q: *This is our final interview so let's talk about you.*

JL: About my tragic life? What do you want to know?

Q: *Well, you've been at Stanford for over thirty years now. How did you get here? Or why did you enter the Jesuits? Or why did you leave? Or whatever you want to talk about. What's your first memory?*

JL: My first memory. I've always wondered whether my first memory was an actual memory or if it was something that my parents talked about and that's what I remember. Because I think I have a clear memory of something that happened when I was less than a year old. Does that seem possible?

My parents had gone off for an overnight in New York—to celebrate a promotion my father got, I'm told—and my brother and I were left in the care of my French grandmother. What I seem to recall is that she didn't much like me. I began to cry and my brother was rocking my crib, I think, and after a while grandma got fed up with my crying and said, "Leave him alone, Jerry. He's a crybaby. Nobody likes a crybaby." And I stopped crying right on the spot. I'd swear I remember it, viscerally as well as literally. I understood that my grandma didn't like me because I was crying, and if I kept on crying nobody else would like me either. I got the message early.

In any case I grew up wanting not to be disliked, something that seemed likely to happen at any minute. I wasn't out to be charming. I just didn't want to do any of those things—like crying—that would make me the child you didn't want to have. That attitude was intensified, I'm sure, by reading a series of little essays my aunt, Sister Mary Sebastian, used to send me called *Saintly Children of Our Own Times.* I read them dutifully when they arrived each month: kid after kid was afflicted with tuberculosis or leukemia or polio—it was mass destruction for the kiddies—and every one of them endured excruciating pain with a heart full of joy and they just couldn't wait to die and be with Jesus. So every month I too wanted to climb onto the funeral pyre, not because I was crazy about Jesus, but so people would say, "Isn't he wonderful!" This attitude carried over, I suppose, until I was 35 or 36 and I left the Jesuits. That's when I got down from the funeral pyre and said, "Thanks very much, but it's simply too hot up there."

Q: *We just went from one year old to thirty-five. Did anything happen in between?*

JL: Not much of interest. I think I was a neurotic child right from the start. I was always terribly concerned to say and do the right thing . . . unlike my brother who was a hellion and always in trouble. He grew up normal. He was always the most popular boy in school. He got lousy grades in grammar school but he was a football player in high school and so he kept his grades high enough to get into college. He was one of those guys who was pursued by all the girls. He hated school but he got a degree in civil engineering—with honors—from Manhattan College. He served in Korea during that war and married immediately after it. Had six kids, one after the other, in the Catholic manner. Normal, all the way through. Except for this: at forty-five, with a wife and six kids, he quit his office job and became a lumberjack. He used his retirement money to buy a chunk of Mt. Tom on the Connecticut River and he logged it successfully for the next fifteen or twenty years, until he retired. And then the federal government bought the property from him in some kind of conservation move. Jerry did very well.

Q: *How much older than you is he?*

JL: He's four years older. He's suffering from two kinds of cancer, and when I told him how sorry I was to know this, he paused for a moment, puzzled, and said, "Hell, you've got to die of something!"

Q: *(Laughs.)*

JL: Normal and brave.

Q: *I would have thought you were an only child.*

JL: A lot of people say that. By which they mean I'm a mess, I suppose.

Q: *Tell me more about being neurotic as a child.*

JL: I'll tell you about when I discovered the pleasures of malice. I was about seven—or maybe eight or nine, who knows?—when I scored a big hit with my parents by imitating the pastor of our church who was a Monsignor and a terrific windbag. I'd puff out my belly and throw back my head and strut around the way he did, talking in a self-important voice, and they would roar with laughter. I guess the imitation was pretty good and, most of all, it was completely unexpected. I had never been funny before. My mother would say, "Isn't that terrible, he's imitating the priest! We shouldn't laugh, but do it just one more time." And I would do it again and again. I realized then that you could get away with all kinds of outrageous things so long as you were funny about it. And that people liked you if you were funny, or at least they excused you for being peculiar. So right from the start I was on the lookout for people to imitate. It made me very aware of what was slightly overdone, what was pretentious, what was pure bullshit. And it was a way of gaining acceptance.

Q: *This plays right into your becoming a writer, a satirist.*

JL: It does, sort of, doesn't it.

Q: *Do you think some people are fated to be writers?*

JL: Maybe. I certainly wasn't. I wanted to be a painter like my cousin John.

Q: *He was a great influence on you?*

JL: Only insofar as he did this thing—painted, invented cartoon strips—that normal kids didn't do. He was the great hero of my childhood. He was much, much older than I and we rarely had any contact since he lived in Springfield and I was in South Hadley, in the boondocks. As it happens, I met him a couple weeks ago in Boston at a family funeral. He's almost completely blind. He's got masses of white hair even now in his 80s. Looks terrific. He was being led by his sister because he can't see well enough to negotiate a graveyard, but I told him that he had been my childhood hero and I gave him a big hug. The poor man pulled back in horror. He couldn't believe he was being hugged by some geriatric case from California. And I realized they still don't hug in Boston.

Q: *You keep moving away from the subject of how you became a writer.*

JL: Well, we've talked about it before, haven't we? I grew up a lonely kid. My brother was four years older than I, and as soon as he hit age thirteen, he disappeared with friends his own age. There were no other kids my age where we lived, so I read and read until I felt provoked to write and then I just kept writing, not as a vocation of any kind but because I liked putting stuff down on paper. Poems. Stories. It's nothing unusual. Every writer goes through that stage. By the time I got to high school I wanted to be an actor. We've talked about that too. My parents and I made a pact that I'd finish college before trying professional acting. My poor parents.

Q: *You've mentioned your parents only briefly. What were they like?*

JL: They were nice; they were hard-working and ambitious for their children; they were gifted, both of them.

Q: *Explain that, if you would: they were gifted.*

JL: I mean that not enough came of their gifts. My mother always felt she was a failure because she had showed enormous talent as a pianist and gave it up without giving it a fair shot. Straight out of high school she was accepted to the New England Conservatory of Music in Boston, went there, and left after two weeks. Or two months, I'm not sure. As I've heard the story, she was eighteen, she knew nobody in Boston, and she was living in a rented room. All alone. But it was the endless hours in the practice studio that did her in. She was too young and inexperienced to be left on her own like that and the loneliness got to be too much. She packed up and went home. I think she always felt it was a major failure both of courage and of stamina. Certainly when I was growing up we never had a piano in the house. I heard her play once at my aunt's house—I must have been nine or ten—and I remember being thrilled by the music and, in a way I didn't understand, proud of her and astonished at her ability. Thinking back now, I can't imagine what a moment of shock it must have been for her to be playing again after so many years. It was the first and last time I ever heard her play.

Mind you, having said all that about failure and frustration, I should correct the impression I'm giving by saying that she was a very funny woman, a terrific mimic and a born comic.

My father was quieter. He had a dry wit and a highly developed sense of irony. He could design and build anything—from fine furniture to elegant houses—and he was a gifted painter though he didn't start painting until he was nearly sixty. At first he took courses at the University of Connecticut and painted the conventional stuff you'd expect of a beginning painter—realism, impressionism, copying the greats—but then suddenly he discovered abstract expressionism and found his real talent. He'd been a civil engineer all his working life, so form and its organization in space came naturally to him. He did some extraordinarily good work. He began late but he lasted long enough to have exhibits at the Berkshire Museum and to see his work admired and bought.

Q: *Why do you think your mother gave up so easily? I don't think you would have.*

JL: No, I wouldn't have. I'd have spent seventeen years trying, making everybody around me miserable, and then I'd have given up. (Laughs.) Actually, I think I understand it. She was the youngest girl in an enormous family and I'm sure she'd been spoiled rotten. She'd never been away from home and nobody else in the family had ever gone on to higher studies of any kind, so the whole enterprise must have been threatening. And then there's the perseverance factor; talent is never enough by itself; you've got to be driven as well. When she left Boston she went back to Springfield and enrolled in secretarial school.

Q: *And your father, you said, was a civil engineer.*

JL: Well, he eventually became a civil engineer; he started out as a carpenter. He dropped out of high school at 16. He was the oldest boy and his parents felt that education was a waste of time and he should help support the family. So he apprenticed as a carpenter and spent years going to night school and eventually he became a job supervisor and finally one of the head engineers in a large construction company. He built a huge hydroelectric plant in the Connecticut River and he was senior engineer for the fortification of Portsmouth Harbor during World War II. By the time he retired he had five M.I.T. grads working under him. He was a remarkable man, self-educated, and a great lover of education. At age sixty he got himself accepted to the MFA program in painting and fine arts at the University of Connecticut.

Q: *And they're both deceased now?*

JL: My father died in November of '85 and my mother died

in January of '86. Three months apart. Horrible deaths. My father lingered for over ten years with Parkinson's disease and my mother took care of him until near the end when she was diagnosed with ALS, Lou Gehrig's disease. So he suffered endless physical debilitation and by the end his mind was beginning to go. My mother's muscles ceased to function one by one. She lost her speech first and then her ability to swallow and at the end her eyelids were taped open for ten minutes at a time so she could see. But her mind remained sharp right to the last day. It's a horrible story, a kind of living entombment for both of them. Old age is a beautiful thing.

Q: *Have you written about this?*

JL: I wrote a novel called *Lies*, which was an attempt to capture something about the complexity of their lives, but it didn't work. Still, I suppose everything I've written is conditioned by their dying, and there's a scene in *An Honorable Profession* where the mother, who has ALS, launches herself from a reclining chair onto her walker, overshoots it, and sprawls on the floor, shaking with laughter. The caregiver, Tillie Columbia, comes rushing into the room and says, "Now look at what you've done!" It's a scene of awful black comedy and of course it happened to my mother in exactly this way—she couldn't speak but she wrote it out for me—and she laughed while she wrote it down. I put it in the novel as a tribute to her courage. She was a great complainer all her life, but once she got her death notice she never complained again. She was heroic in the last years of her life.

My brother was flipping through *An Honorable Profession* one day—until then he had never read any of my books—and he saw a reference to Lou Gehrig's disease and he stopped to read it. He read this particular scene, first with horror—"he's writing about our mother!"—and then with great amusement, because he could see the indomitable old girl lying on the floor and laughing at what a good story it was going to make. He then went back and read the book right from the start. He got hooked and read all my books from *Tight White Collar* on. "I've read them all now," he said to me. He shook his head, a little saddened. "I had no idea you were such an unhappy man."

Q: *"All happy families are the same; each unhappy family is unhappy in its own way. "*

JL: Exactly. There's no conflict in fiction until things begin to go wrong.

My parents were generous and supportive; the one thing they wanted for us was a good education. Of course like all parents what they most wanted for their children were two things: they want you to be happy and they want you never to die. Alas, nobody gets out alive.

Actually, I wasn't a planned baby. They didn't want me at first.

Q: *That comes out of nowhere. Should I ask you to talk about that or should I just pass on to some other topic?*

JL: I brought it up so I guess I must want to talk about it. I think that knowing I was not wanted has probably conditioned who I've been for the past seventy years.

This is how I understand it. My parents married on November 11, 1929 and when they got back from their honeymoon they were welcomed into the Great Depression. Before their marriage my father had had a good job and there had been lots of available cash—apparently everybody spent everything they earned in those heady days—and they had no reason to think it wouldn't always be this way. But suddenly they discovered my father had been laid off, since of course construction was the first thing to stop in the Depression. My mother continued to work for a short while and then she too was laid off. By the end of the first year of marriage they had a baby. It was a breech birth. The doctor was a great believer in the virtues of waiting, so he didn't bother to turn the baby. My mother was in labor for two days and she was just about torn apart. It sounds inhuman today but somehow she and the baby survived. She was in the hospital for over a month and, though they loved my brother, another birth was something neither of them wanted to repeat. So four years later when they found out she was pregnant, they were appalled. My mother was convinced she could never survive another baby and my father was haunted by guilt, so right up to the last minute my arrival was greeted with dread. And with loathing, I imagine.

I found out about this in just the way you'd suppose: I overheard a conversation when my mother was playing bridge with some women friends. They were talking about pregnancy and she told the ghastly story of my brother's birth and then added, "So when I was pregnant the second time, we didn't want the baby at all, and it was such a relief when Jackie was born because the birth was so easy." This conversation, by the way, took place at a time when she was thrilled at being pregnant with another child, eight years my junior. She miscarried, as it happens, so there's just my brother and me. But I had heard that conversation and knew that I hadn't been wanted. I remember thinking of it as an intellectual issue: they didn't want me before I was born, but now they do; isn't that interesting? Later, in high school, I remember thinking that's why I always felt out of place everywhere, not knowing what to say, not knowing what to do, not knowing how to fit in. It was a comfort, in some perverse way, to think I was never comfortable anywhere because nobody wanted me in the first place. Of course it doesn't really matter if you were wanted or not; if you feel you weren't, the damage is done. A no-fault accident.

Q: *Is that why you became a Jesuit?*

JL: Who could say? Maybe. Certainly I was bothered by God right from the start. I can remember as a child of nine or ten going to mass and being fascinated by the scripture readings because they told these improbable—and clearly unfair—stories. I remember being outraged particularly by the prodigal son. I immediately identified with the older son, the good one who stayed home and worked in the fields while the other brother, the hellion, went out and had a good time for himself and spent all his money on prostitutes and then when he came home, destitute, they threw him a party and gave him a ring and a fatted calf. And I thought, Of course, Jerry would get the party and I'd get the shaft. I remember talking about it at home and saying how unfair it was. My mother said, "It only seems unfair. It's God's way of forgiving." And I said, "But it is unfair. The older one did what he was supposed to do and he didn't get a party. He didn't get anything. And the younger one got everything. Why should that be?" And she said, "Well, that's how it is. That's just how God is." (Laughs.) She was puzzled too but she was willing to accept it whereas I had my doubts. Then there were all those other parables about the unprofitable servant, the cursed fig tree, the workers who showed up at the eleventh hour and got full pay, the invitee to the wedding banquet who got thrown out because he didn't have a wedding garment, the unprofitable servant, the foolish virgins. God seemed to me utterly unreasonable and we were supposed to love him. No wonder I was more interested in the Saintly Children of Our Own Times.

What was the question again, please?

Q: *Is that why you became a Jesuit?*

JL: Right. That lovely question. I got through high school with no intention whatsoever of being a priest of any kind, and at college the only thing I wanted to do was act. Holy Cross wasn't much of a college at the time—it could boast Bob Cousy and Tommy Heinsohn and a fabulous NCAA basketball team—but intellectually it was second rate. For me, however it was great. It was the start of a social life. For the first time since Billy Muir I had friends, lots of them, and I spent most of my time goofing off. Then in my second year I got derailed by Jesus. Who knows how or why?

I remember I was talking with one of my roommates about being an actor, and out of nowhere he said, "Why don't you become a priest. You're smart enough. You have no moral impediments"—he talked like that—"and it's something positive and useful you could do with your life instead of wasting it as an actor." I dismissed what he said as ridiculous, but at the moment he said it, I knew it was going to change my life. Nonetheless I went ahead and spent forty dollars on head shots for my acting portfolio but at the end of that year I entered the Jesuits. I was nineteen.

Q: *And that's when you began to take writing seriously?*

JL: Hardly. That was when I began to take Latin and Greek seriously.

Q: *I don't know if it's okay to ask this, but I'll risk it: what made you want to be a priest and what made you leave the priesthood?*

JL: Got a minute? I suppose the short answer for why I became a priest is the one I give in *Picnic in Babylon.* It was a decision based almost solely on reason: it seemed to me the best thing I could do with my life, there were no convincing reasons not to do it, and so I did it. That makes me sound like some kind of automaton, and in a way I suppose I was, but there had to be a lot of emotional and psychological factors that figured into the decision as well. You can't discount the influence of those Saintly Children and their eagerness to give up everything—including their lives—to please Jesus and at the same time to get it all over with. I did fancy the idea of being dead to the world. What kind of lunacy was that?

Q: *Was it lunacy? What was life with the Jesuits like?*

JL: It was like life in the sixteenth century, I suppose. I entered the Jesuits in 1954 when the course of studies was essentially the same as it had been for hundreds of years. There was a two-year novitiate period during which you studied ascetical theology, Latin and Greek, and spent the rest of your time meditating on the life of Christ and the

Jesuit Rules. It was an intense exposure to the spiritual life and, if you were approved at the end of it, you took vows of poverty, chastity, and obedience. It's a fairly usual approach to the religious life; you'd find something similar in the Franciscans or the Dominicans or any other religious order.

Q: *It sounds pretty distant from ordinary college life. How did you take to it?*

JL: I remember waking my first morning in a vast room with thirty other Postulants and thinking, "My God, what kind of horrible mistake is this!" But I got to like the disciplined nature of the life. We weren't allowed to speak in the house unless it was absolutely necessary and, when we did speak, it had to be in Latin. I liked that. I had sort of faked my way through five years of Latin in high school and college, so it was nice to learn the language at last, and I still sometimes read it for pleasure before bed. Catullus, mostly, but also Horace; mostly the stuff I taught as a Jesuit.

Q: *So what happens after you take vows?*

JL: Oh, yes, the fifteen year course of studies. After vows you spend two years studying the Greek and Roman classics, three years studying philosophy (largely Thomistic, but modern philosophers as well), three years teaching in one of the Jesuit high schools, four years studying theology, and then a final year of ascetical theology in which you recapitulate the experience of your original two-year novitiate. Fifteen years in all. Then you can begin working on a Ph.D. in your particular specialty. Mine was English literature.

Q: *And did you tell me once that all these courses are taught in Latin?*

JL: Yes, the textbooks were in Latin—they were the prof's Xeroxed notes, mostly—and the lectures were in Latin and the hour oral at the end of each year was in Latin. I was lucky because my spoken Latin was pretty good and it enabled me to conceal how little I knew about philosophy.

Q: *Can you still speak Latin?*

JL: Well, it's been a long time since I've had to, but I can muster the odd phrase. My grammar is shot to hell by now and any fluency I had is pretty much gone. Let's just say I used to be able to speak Latin. It's not an issue that comes up very often.

Q: *I don't think you said at what point during these fifteen years you actually become a priest.*

JL: You get ordained after your third year of theology, at the end of your thirteenth year. After that you go out to parishes every weekend, saying mass and hearing confessions and so forth like any parish priest, except on Monday you're back in class preparing for your final exams and writing a thesis on something theological. I wrote on St. Anselm's Ontological Argument for the Existence of God. Hot stuff.

Q: *So you remain attached to your own monasteries or schools. You don't have your own parishes?*

JL: Right. You always remain attached to some Jesuit community, usually a college or a high school or a mission. I was a New England Jesuit and one of our mission stations was Baghdad. We've been thrown out of Iraq, of course. Our college and high school there were nationalized after the murder of King Faisal and it wasn't long before the Jesuits were expelled altogether. The Baghdad University building you see on television all the time was built by the Jesuits. It was a great mission.

Q: *Did you ever want to be a missionary?*

JL: No, but of course I'd have gone if they sent me. There's a story about three reluctant missionaries who were being seen off by their Superior who blessed their farewell with the traditional invocation, "Vade in pace, in nomine Jesu Christi"—"Go in peace in the name of Christ"—which they in their misery chose to translate as "For Chrissake, go quietly." (I guess it's funnier if you know Latin.) But for the most part you weren't sent to the missions unless you specifically requested it. Which was lucky for me. I had a hard enough time just getting through the course of studies. I don't think I'd ever have survived in Baghdad.

Q: *Well, fifteen years is a very long time. Do the Jesuits still do that?*

JL: Actually, no. That all changed shortly after Vatican II. I was in the last class to go through the whole fifteen year course, with Latin a constant and with terrific concentration on Thomism and the philosophical problems of earlier centuries. I think that now they accept only college grads and the course of study itself is about half as long. And, I imagine, twice as effective.

Q: *What is your feeling about all those years you spent studying? You sound as if you feel it was a bad investment of time. Surely there must have been pleasant experiences—intellectual pleasures—that kept you going?*

JL: Oh, those were real pleasures and they were considerable. I have to admit that philosophy was a total loss for me; I regret those three years of study, though I did manage to write a lot of poetry. Theology was a different matter. I was interested in theology.

Q: *Let's stick to philosophy for a moment. You're saying you didn't like philosophy?*

JL: The way a philosopher thinks is by its nature opposed to the way a fiction writer must think. I really believe that.

Q: *Explain that, will you?*

JL: Philosophy moves from the particular to the abstract on its way toward universal truths, whereas fiction is concerned with the practical, the concrete. Philosophy wants to investigate eternal questions such as whether or not we can know anything for certain and, if so, how? These are fascinating questions, but they don't make for fiction, which wants to know who this particular man is and how he thinks and acts, and why.

Q: *What about philosophical novelists?*

JL: The more philosophical they are, the less engaging they're likely to be, I think. There's Gide, Joyce, and Mann, and you certainly have to regard them as philosophical novelists, but don't you agree that each of them is more admired for his fiction than for the philosophical questions he raises? I've never known anybody who reads Joyce for his philosophy. But then there's Sartre and Camus, whom you do read for their philosophy, but they make it worth your while. Camus is a wonderful novelist. *The Stranger* is a fascinating book and it's certainly the fictional embodiment of an existential issue, but in general I think it's true that the more philosophical the work, the less impressive it is as fiction.

Q: *Okay. You're saying that philosophy is concerned with the pursuit of truth with a capital T whereas fiction is concerned with a particular truth of everyday experience . . . which may reflect something larger, but in itself it's not concerned with abstractions.*

JL: Exactly. But the real danger is the habit of mind. The habit of speculating philosophically is opposed by its nature to the fictional process of observing the way somebody curls his lip as he puts out his cigarette, a gesture that may turn out to be trace evidence, say, of an act of violence. The fiction writer must be an observer. He has to see. "One of those on whom nothing is lost." James.

Q: *Is this resistance to philosophy common among fiction writers?*

JL: Probably not. I imagine most fiction writers like to think of themselves as philosophical. It makes them sound deep. Of course they haven't spent three full years of their lives studying Thomistic philosophy. In Latin.

Q: *So you didn't like philosophy, you said, but you did like theology. What did you like most about being a priest?*

JL: I didn't like preaching and I wasn't keen on the mind-set of the Vatican, but I was good at hearing confessions. I was lucky in having a great moral theology professor who insisted that confession was between God and the penitent and it was the priest's job to be there to help. People who bother to come to confession are, almost without exception, good people who feel they have failed at some moral obligation and want to set things right. In my time as a priest—the late 1960s—the big problem was birth control. The Pope had spoken out against it but the Vatican Council had insisted on the primacy of conscience. So I would try to instruct penitents—women, almost always—that the practice of birth control was a matter of conscience and I'd run through three questions to help them form their conscience. That scene in the first section of *The Miracle* is pretty much how I handled it. Do you know the section I mean? Shall I read it to you? I've got it right here.

Q: *Read it.*

JL: There's a priest, Fr. Boyle, who is quizzing LeBlanc on how he handles birth control issues in confession. This is what LeBlanc says:

> "I tell them they should ask themselves three questions. Like this. I say: 'First, you should ask yourself if you are shirking your Christian responsibilities; that is to say, "Do I just want the pleasures of sex without the responsibility of children?" Now you've already got two children, you said, so obviously you're not out just for pleasure.' Or, if they don't have any children, I say, 'Probably you'll want to have children later, someday.' Anyway, I take away their worry about the sex part. Then I say, 'Second, you ask yourself if there is some real need for you to use birth control. But you've already indicated financial reasons—or psychological or physical, or whatever.' I just fit the answer to the case, you see. Then, 'Third, you should ask yourself if this is going to help you and your spouse to lead a fuller, happier, more responsible Christian life. Now, only you and your spouse together can answer that, so you should have a discussion with him or her, then once you've made up your mind to use or not to use birth control, just go ahead and live comfortably with your decision. And whatever you do, don't mention it in confession again, because eventually you're sure to run into some crazy

priest who'll scream and yell and say you're committing mortal sin."'

Q: *I can hear your voice in that passage. Did you really talk like that in confession?*

JL: A little more formally, I think. I left out the crazy priest stuff and the screaming and yelling.

Q: *Is this accepted Church doctrine now?*

JL: It's accepted practice, though I can't think it's approved by the Vatican. The laity, as the rest of us are called, seems to have accepted birth control as a fact. It should be a matter of individual conscience.

Q: *And that other delicate question, if I may: why did you leave?*

JL: Again, I'll give you the answer I always give. Being a priest was too hard for me. I didn't leave because I was disappointed in the Jesuits or in the Church or because I had doctrinal issues. I left because it was too hard to be the kind of priest I wanted to be and it was too important to do any other way. That sounds formulaic, and I suppose it is since it's the answer I always give, and of course there were other factors as well: the vow of chastity, naturally, and the vow of obedience. And I wanted to write.

Q: *But you were writing a lot when you were still a Jesuit, isn't that right?*

JL: Yes, I published a lot of poetry as a Jesuit. Four books, in fact. And *Picnic in Babylon*, as well. But that was well along in my course of studies, and at first my Jesuit superiors were highly suspicious of poetry. Remember, this was the time of Daniel Berrigan, S.J., and his anti-war followers who raided draft boards and encouraged draft resisters and who brought a lot of negative government attention to the Jesuit order. He was already ordained and a distinguished poet as well, so they put up with him, grudgingly in most cases. But I was nobody, a Jesuit in training, and they distrusted my publishing poetry in *Atlantic* instead of in some Jesuit magazine. They feared I'd grow up and turn into another raving liberal like Berrigan. My writing was frowned upon, to say the least. I remember—it was during my philosophy years—an otherwise wonderful, kind superior telling me, "Don't waste too much time on that poetry. That's not what you're here for." I also remember a not very nice superior telling me, "We're watching you every second. We know you write poetry and we know you publish it. So you'd better be sure you keep in line." He was an interesting man, six feet seven, completely devoid of a sense of humor. He was known, unkindly, as The Tower of Power and The Spire of Ire. As you can tell from that alone, I had problems with charity as well as with the vows.

Q: *And so you left.*

JL: Yes, but only after trying it out for seventeen years. I should say before we leave this topic that I'm eternally grateful to the Jesuits for two things. They gave me an education beyond anything I could ever have dreamed of. And I made friendships there that have lasted all my life, brilliant and gifted men whom I love and admire. Interestingly enough, most of my closest friends have stayed. They're still Jesuits. The proof of a real vocation.

Q: *You went to Harvard for your Ph. D. while you were still a Jesuit. Did that seem strange to you?*

JL: It was wonderful. Harvard at that time was extremely unwelcoming to its graduate students—at least to the ones in English—so there were some unhappy people, but we were all thrilled to be there and to be with each other, despite the general feeling of insecurity. I was ten years older than most of the others and I had published four books, so I didn't need a lot of coddling. Besides, I lucked into meeting a couple professors who have remained friends, one of whom was Al Gelpi who left Harvard in '69 to come to Stanford. I took his seminar in Ezra Pound, the best class I ever had. He and his wife Barbara became my friends there at Harvard and we remain friends still. But the truth is that

I was tired to death of studying—it was my 29th successive year in school—and I just couldn't take the Ph.D. as seriously as I should have. Then a nice thing happened. There I was in my mid-thirties working on the Great American Term Paper and tired of being a student when I was invited to a cocktail party at *Atlantic* and my life changed forever.

Robert Manning, the editor in chief, had read the galleys of *Picnic in Babylon* and wanted to excerpt a section for the magazine. They had been publishing my poetry for years and for some reason they thought I was an old man. So they were surprised at *Picnic*, and out of nowhere Manning said, "It's a fascinating story. Why are you working for a Ph.D.? Why don't you come work for us instead?" It seemed to me preposterous, but a year later I dropped out of Harvard and did just that. I gather I was sort of a gamble on Manning's part, but after two months I became a Staff Editor with my name on the masthead.

Q: *That's almost unbelievable, to become an editor at a major magazine with no previous publishing experience.*

JL: I know. Manning was a very unconventional editor. He took chances on people and in this instance I was supremely lucky. Actually, I think he was rather intrigued by the idea of hiring a Jesuit priest as an editor at a magazine that had once been quite anti-Catholic. So I went to work for *Atlantic* where I had first look at the poetry and fiction and whatever lit. crit. came along. The magazine was just then becoming the very political magazine it is today, and there were political figures as well as famous writers coming in and out the doors, so it was an exciting place to be. I loved working there and I got myself a tiny apartment and I lived happily ever after. For a year and a half. During that time I continued to go out to parishes for weekend mass and confessions, but more and more I felt my priestly life was being subsumed by my job at the magazine. I finally became sufficiently uncomfortable with the secular-sacred duality of my life to tell my superiors that I wanted to leave *Atlantic* to go live in London and make a final decision about whether or not to remain a Jesuit and a priest. They were very understanding, probably because they had seen this coming for some time.

Q: *Why London?*

Q: Because I didn't know anybody there and I figured I'd be able to make up my mind without any personal distractions whatsoever, no kindly advice, no helpful suggestions, no pressure of any kind. And it worked. I went to mass every day and prayed about what I should do and in less than three months I decided to leave. It wasn't an easy decision, especially since it affected other people as well as me. Nobody is pleased to see you fail at something and that's what I was doing. None of my superiors was surprised. My parents were surprised, however, but in their typical generous fashion they remained completely supportive. They were behind me in whatever I decided to do. Later, when I married, they welcomed Joan as if she was the best thing that had ever entered our lives--perhaps because she was—and they never showed any sign of disappointment in my failure as a priest.

Q: *Do you still regard it as a failure?*

JL: Oh yes. That's what it was. I had made vows of poverty, chastity, and obedience and I had been ordained a priest and now I was asking out of my vows. It's a complicated process. You can't be un-ordained, so according to Church law I am still a priest. I'm just not allowed to do any priestly work. We still have no married clergy.

Q: *And then you married Joan?*

JL: I had met Joan at Harvard in the late '60s; we were married in '71. She wasn't the reason I left the priesthood, though of course she was in the background, maybe the foreground, of my decision. I had met her as a grad student when she was finishing a degree in education. She had been a nun in the School Sisters of Notre Dame for some fifteen years, so we had a common background and an easy understanding of where we'd been and where we wanted to go. Meeting her was the best thing that ever happened to me.

Q: *That's nice.*

JL: She's nice.

Q: *So you married and came to Stanford. How did that come about?*

JL: In the usual way. I applied, the chairman of the search committee liked my resume, they interviewed me, and I got the job.

Q: *It was that easy?*

JL: I've left out all the interesting stuff. It was a mini blood letting. Albert Guerard, who was the great man in the English Department and the great opponent of Wally Stegner, made this the final issue of their long power struggle. Albert insisted that I was just one more of that pallid, east coast, Harvard set who wrote the same old fashioned prose that was killing literature and what we needed to replace Wally—he had retired a year earlier—was someone experimental and daring and cutting edge. Somebody who wrote books without punctuation or—like Perec—without the letter e. One of his protégées, for instance, by the name of Clive Miller. So the department was soon divided between Miller and me. I had the advantage because by this time I had published 6 books with another about to come out and Clive hadn't published any fiction at all. It was a bitter, angry battle between the two factions. And once again I was supremely lucky. I got the job. Incidentally Albert and I became good friends over the years and, when I finally got to meet Clive Miller, I found him smart and funny and charming. He just wasn't as lucky as I.

Q: *Shall we talk some more about the writing program?*

JL: We've talked about it enough, haven't we?

Q: *Well, I'm curious about how you respond to somebody else running what you must regard as your writing program.*

JL: Oh, that's easy to talk about. Eavan Boland runs the program, and has for over ten years now, and she's the best thing that's happened to it since Wallace Stegner. Wally founded it. I made it an all-Fellowship program. But Eavan has expanded and enriched it beyond anything I could imagine.

She's responsible for our getting the Stein Visiting Writer in Fiction and the Mohr Visiting Writer in Poetry—both of these with a huge endowment, by the way—and she's added a Creative Writing Minor to our course offerings and she's expanded our actual enrollment to the point where sixty percent of students in the English Department have a concentration in Creative Writing. She serves on nearly every major committee in the University and gives an air of credibility and importance to the Program itself. We're taken seriously by the Dean's Office, the Provost's Office, and—perhaps most important—by the English Department. There's none of that condescension toward creative writing that you find at most major universities.

The best part, and the thing I most applaud, is that everything she does and all the money she raises is for the Fellows. In the years that she's been Director, she's devised ways of giving them all kinds of teaching opportunities, she's arranged for them to have summers off with a handsome honorarium, and she's more than doubled their monthly stipend. Their well-being is her constant concern.

She's also a major contemporary poet by the way.

Q: *In Ireland, I understand, as well as in the States.*

JL: In the English speaking world. She's the real thing.

Q: *So you like her personally as well as professionally.*

JL: I also admire her. And if I still have the feeling that it's my Program—and I confess that sometimes I do—I also have the feeling that it's in very safe hands.

Q: *A last word about writing in general? Your own writing?*

JL: Done. Except for my Italian novel.

Q: *And what do you have to say about that?*

JL: Absolutely nothing. I don't want to jinx it.

Q: *But this is a huge departure for you, I imagine. You've never written an historical novel, have you?*

JL: I couldn't write it if I thought it was an historical novel. It's just another novel that happens to require a lot of historical research.

Q: *What about the old adage that says you should write about what you know? I wonder what you think of that?*

JL: I've never believed that. You don't write about what you know. You write about the things you don't know about what you know. What you know is the subject of your life: yourself, your spouse, your friends . . . and then something mysterious happens with a spouse or a friend. They do something or say something that is totally out of character and you try to put that together with what you know about them and it doesn't fit. You discover that this person you thought you knew is in fact unknown and perhaps unknowable . . . and that's what you write about, that mystery. If you just write about what you know, you end up writing a Hollywood sit-com, I should imagine.

Q: *So for you writing is a process that attempts to answer or discover?*

JL: To discover. Right. You invent something, in the double sense of making something up and discovering something that's already there.

Q: *So truth can be reached only tangentially, as Simone de Beauvoir says.*

JL: I didn't know Simone said that but good old Simone is right. Newspapers deal with facts; they try to report the facts accurately; they're concerned with the representation of things as they are. Fiction deliberately distorts things as they are in order to get at a larger truth.

Can we stop now?

Q: *Are we ready? Do we know all we should know about your life?*

JL: All that's fit to print. I hope.

Q: *Nothing else?*

JL: You might want to know what Joan has promised to put on my tombstone. It hits me off perfectly I think.

Q: *Let's hear it.*

JL: "Here lie the ashes of John L'Heureux.
He suffered no pain without complaint."

Q: *(Laughs.)*

JL: Absolutely right and carved in stone.

SELECTED REVIEWS OF L'HEUREUX'S FICTION

Tight White Collar
untitled

John L'Heureux's first novel, *Tight White Collar*, is a tense, fast-moving narration of one day in the life of Ransom, a highly intelligent and liberal member of the Society of Jesus. Ransom is a dissenter, a follower of Pope John and Vatican II, who hopes to bring about change "within the system." He seems to oscillate between the extremes of a compulsive piety and a secretly cynical irony, and this emotional tightrope act helps him come to terms with the Pauline bureaucracy of the church. The texture of L'Heureux's style—the naturalistic immediacy shot through with occasional patches of Joycean interior monologue—enables the author to transubstantiate Ransom's experiences into metaphors of a divided sensibility.

This division, this hidden inauthenticity, is suddenly exposed when Ransom is forced to return home for the funeral of Bernie, his Protestant brother-in-law. The dogmatic certitudes and polarities of Catholicism—which Ransom (who, like John L'Heureux before he left the order, is a well-known "underground" priest) has never really questioned—begin to crumble under the pressure of this confrontation with the Other. On his way home, Ransom is swamped by the contingency that overwhelmed Roquentin in Sartre's *Nausea*. As he reads his breviary on the train, he considers how ugly, menacing, and undignified the people around him appear. They seem very much like personifications of "the snake that stops its ears," that demonic and unredeemable evil which has haunted Catholicism for centuries, causing the church and its philosophers to hunger greedily for transcendence. And yet, Ransom wonders, isn't the serpent of quotidian chaos and uncertainty far less evil than the self-righteous wrath of the Elect?

This questioning gains momentum after Ransom arrives home for the funeral. Although he maintains his priestly demeanor at his parents' home and among the Protestants at the funeral, he begins to see beneath the pieties and petty frauds that have formed the basis of his family relationships. Some of the dialogue in these scenes, as well as the Robbe-Grillet-like memory flashes, is amateurish and mechanical, but the overall pattern rings astonishingly true. Especially admirable is L'Heureux's narration of Ransom's funeral oration, which counterpoints the words of St. Paul with Ransom's *sotto voce* questioning of those very words:

That passage from St. Paul, he thought, doesn't prove a damned thing. All it says is that if Christ isn't risen, then our faith is not well founded. Well, maybe it's *not* well founded. Maybe we *are* wrong and this whole business is just a gigantic charade. God's little joke. God's sick joke. I must be losing my mind. I do believe. Help thou my unbelief....

Death is the muse of poetry, said Schopenhauer, and Jesuit-trained revolutionaries from Hopkins to Joyce to L'Heureux have had to come to terms with a death wish concealed within the edifice constructed by Paul and Aquinas. It's no accident that the Jesuits, created as a kind of Waffen SS to beat back the heresies of the Reformation, have in fact spawned some of Western civilization's greatest heretics. Stephen Dedalus escaped from the dogma of Aquinas by uniting himself with Leopold Bloom, the despised Other whom the church had for so long repressed (and secretly loved, just as Hitler secretly loved his supposedly Jewish grandfather). Thus Ransom, during the return trip that comprises the last section of *Tight White Collar*, begins to understand that people on the train—the grotesque sandwich-man, the hippies, the noisy children—are like gargoyles on a Gothic cathedral, symbols of the human reality that Christian love has always viewed with the most intense form of hatred.

Before his journey is over, a final, ambiguous revelation catapults Ransom beyond Catholicism into a dialectical consciousness that is at once older than the Church and new. For the sense of a rebellious dialectic that concludes *Tight White Collar* is common to both the critical intransigence of Job and the "permanent revolution" of the present-day people of China.

—John W. Hughes
1972

Clang Birds
From Celibacy to Commitment

"The Clang Bird is a rare creature that flies in ever-decreasing circles at ever increasing speeds until with a terrible clang, it disappears up its own ass. It is only because of the will of God that the Clang Bird is not extinct."—St. Gommer, 1717 Novissima Verba

The above fictive aphorism is the basis for the joke-lesson John L'Heureux, poet, novelist, and ex-Jesuit, is playing on all of us with this novel about the boomerang effect of good intentions. According to the cover blurb, *The Clang Birds* is a "savage, satirical novel about the bright young people of the Christian antiwar movement." The Clang Bird view of man, for the purposes of the novel, was the deathbed utterance of St. Gommer, the founder of an elitist and scholarly Catholic order called the Thomasites. Their intellects trained by holy and learned men in every field of science, their spirits tutored in the virtues of chastity and humility, and their will trained in absolute obedience, the Thomasites bear an unsurprising resemblance to the order L'Heureux has himself left.

At the book's start each of the theological students we meet has one foot in the Church and the other dangling dangerously above treacherous worldly ground. The particular super-serious nuns and priests are scholars at an unnamed university (Harvard) in Cambridge. Intensely uncertain about moral truths, they are nonetheless intensely garrulous and high-minded in their fruitless discussions of their dilemma. Together they argue earnestly in pungent slang and dusty religiosities about how to perform "relevantly" in their vocation, while privately each is on the verge of some flowering of sexuality, the expression of which is doubly prurient and titillating to the reader because of the religious taboo. L'Heureux would have us believe that this group of committed celibates is trying hard not to think about the same thing I often have to try hard not to think about when I first meet one of them.

On this private sexual front, we find Reverend Father George St. George discovering his relentless genital interest in Natalie, a Jewish graduate student of history. Alone in his room one night, George tormentedly looks in the mirror and thrusts his pelvis forward saying "cock," trying to rid himself of the modesty he's acquired during his religious training. In the next split second, he decides to break off with Natalie, because sex is sinful for a priest. That night she will tell him their relationship is immoral, not as he says because sex is sinful, but because they are not in love. Still later the same evening, George will hold a souvenir silver dagger to his throat, again watching himself in his mirror. But when a small drop of blood appears, he will cry and resolve to live. Natalie will become the first of a long string of women who will help him entice himself away from the Church.

George's near-tragedy is paralleled by that of Hans Berger, more a leitmotif than a fleshed-out character. Berger takes secret showers in icy water, singing Ave Maria, and then he chants Hail Marys while he touches his toes, vainly struggling against masturbation. Even confession provides him with little relief since the bored priest tells him his behavior is probably natural.

Then there's sister Imelda, who believes she is only interested in radical Christianity—priests and nuns working together for the underprivileged, for peace, and the Church. But midway through the novel she abandons her nun's role to become wantonly involved with a coal-black Lebanese who believes solely in sensuality. We observe her uneasiness early in the book when she's flying to the Moratorium with the young and charming priest Reginald Body. Sister Imelda is desperately trying not to notice that fair-haired and white-skinned Reginald looks precisely like an ice cream cone. On his part he notices that she has done something to get rid of the mustache on her upper lip and has abandoned her veil and habit. "I feel more like a woman this way," she says, gazing at him despairingly.

A more macabre voyeurism was my reaction to reading about the familiar political activities of this group and the more exotic theology that gets them there. I am touched and entranced by the systematic moral system these people erect and their inevitable struggle to live within it, alongside the hedonism and styleless anarchy that is our contemporary culture. Their political struggles begin when Reginald suggests out of petty pique for something else that they move into a ghetto and become radical Christians, doing good works. Startling themselves, they agree. Soon they've organized a menage in an old dilapidated house on Oak Street in a working-class Catholic neighborhood, and while consuming great quantities of booze, they ponder how they will do good in the neighborhood and in passing discover they like one another. After forming a radical group called Lollypops, they search for a just cause to uphold. When a university building burns down, their purpose emerges: the university must make the building a center for the Somerville area's poor residents, rather than a pristine museum to high culture.

At first, the protest march reads like instant nostalgia. Like a hundred such rallies, it is half picnic and half desperation; the double picket line giving participants a chance to talk to friends they rarely see except on such occasions. I read about it with the ambivalence of a one-time participant, ashamed of the small concerns and the self-conscious pridefulness, yet proud of them as I was once proud of myself. At least, no matter how absurd, they were standing up for counting. Then of course, L'Heureux's art takes over the narrative. After the enthusiasm of the marchers starts to wane, they look for means of sustaining the crowd. No, they decide, they will not bait the cops or destroy the crane poised ready to demolish the building's smoky hulk. Suddenly an emaciated graduate student (whom Sister Imelda recognizes as a fellow student in her creative Christianity class) grabs her sign ("The play's not the thing") instructs someone to release a balloon every 30 seconds, and sprints to the crane and starts to climb its steel struts. It is clear to the ecstatic crowd that he is going to plant the sign on the wrecking ball of the crane. The police helplessly finger their revolvers as he turns and gives them the peace sign. Then, 50 feet in the air, he loses his footing, gives a small scream, and plummets to the rocky ground beneath. The Lollypops agree afterward that the incident is better not talked about. However, their zeal is not daunted, and in pursuit of good works they wreck the records of an induction center, feeling silly, scared, and only randomly heroic.

The group never manages to cultivate its garden. Mistrusted and despised by their working-class neighbors for being communists (the FBI is tapping their phone), anti-religious (they never seem to attend church), and sybarites (they buy enormous quantities of food and liquor), the Lollypops give a party for the neighbors that is boycotted. Their attempts to make friends with their neighbors result in the use of their basement for sexual exploration and dynamite-making by two young bullies who live next door and who ultimately blow the building up. The young religious scholars succeed only, in fact, in making a few steps toward personal self-realization, moving fearfully or desperately away from the Church. In his deft narrative style, which previews a time after that of the book and explodes into mindless tragedies with the swiftness of a cyclone, L'Heureux shows us that each nun and priest is slowly finding a place in the world, based more on an understanding of what gives him pleasure in life. This is a marked contrast to their often dreamy-eyed, barren, or elitist decisions to enter the Church.

Why is this a good book? On the most basic entertainment level, only where there are taboos can there be agony and prurience about sexual matters. With irony and flair, L'Heureux paints the sexual temptations and realizations of these young adults. They are wrestling with the sinfulness of violating a final taboo. Here are adults whom the very act of sex makes vibrate consciously with a greater eternal agony than even the most fearful adulterer can allow himself to feel.

Second, the tightly plotted political activities of the group are a glimpse into a private world cluttered with high moral precepts which are often the impetus to trivial actions or blunders. Translating abstract notions of good into specific acts of activity that only the most foolish and at the same time respectable among us can dare. L'Heureux has spun a contemporary morality tale about people trying to live by absolutist standards in an era in which relativity and moral chaos are the closest things to standards we have.

—Susan Braudy
1973

Family Affairs
Priests and Victims

In John L'Heureux's "Fox and Swan," a story first collected in *Best Short Stories of 1972,* a character insists, "In the human reaction to...inhuman cold there must be a story." *Family Affairs,* L'Heureux's first collection of short stories explores this theme in depth. A former priest himself, he looks for the proof of his hypothesis primarily in the lives of priests, both former and present, whose own sins prove as damning as those of the cold-hearted lay folk who surround them. These often highly ironic portraits are among the most skillful in the collection.

"The Innocents," for example, excels as pure comic fun, but L'Heureux will not leave his story without its point. A snobbish but handsome Thomasite novice doubling as a parochial school English teacher arouses the immature passions of one of his students. The girl's mother discovers the secret by prying into the wild fantasies revealed in her daughter's diary. Desperate with longing, the girl resolves to expose her love—literally—by offering herself, half-naked, to her teacher at a school dance. But between her mother's almost vengeful spying and the priest's ignorance and fright at her behavior, the girl is trapped, a victim of cold self-absorbtion.

The victim

At the center of each of L'Heureux's stories lies a victim, someone who through no apparent fault of his own is forced by degrees to a dead-end wall of desperation. In "Something Missing" a musical prodigy commits suicide after the torments of parents, teachers, and peers alike lead him to a sense of personal doom. "A Family Affair" chronicles the case history of a poverty-stricken young woman's lesson in suffering as she grows from optimism to a fatalistic acceptance of her plight. In these stories L'Heureux challenges the audience to react humanly in the face of "inhuman cold."

Finally, and most importantly, L'Heureux's explorations of the human soul wracked by cruelty and indifference lead him to the solitary man's dilemma of faith. L'Heureux's priests constantly find their collars tight around their necks. They shift uncertainly between a faith in God and one based in what L'Heureux sees as the life-renewing acts of human contact and the shared appreciation of the wonders of the world.

L'Heureux's talents are more than adequate to the tasks he sets himself. His style blends authority and grace with a shrewd sense of dramatic invention that assures the reader well paced and interesting stories. One story builds on another, and all that spoils a consecutive reading of these tales is L'Heureux's habit of coupling his favorite themes with his favorite story formulae.

The formula

Too many stories begin by describing the story's ending, then flash back to the events leading to the conclusion. L'Heureux's vantage point never departs from that of a distant third person so godly that he does not balk at his own intrusions into the story's action. Finally, L'Heureux becomes so involved with the machinery of his stories—with the business of making plot move logically to their conclusions—that he fails to more than lightly sketch his characters and the stories' settings. At his worst, the characters are wooden, seeming interchangeable in both the cities and the stories they inhabit.

More than anything else though, L'Heureux is a creator of moments. He prefers his characters to witness rather than to personally experience events. And while the role of obstrver[sic] breed distance author, character, and audience alike, it is precisely this distance that fascinates L'Heureux. His interest lies not so much in the simple actions themselves as in the human reactions they elicit. Whether the incident is slight or traumatic, L'Heureux uses it for one purpose—to create a single luminous moment that will bring a story, a life, into focus.

—Diane J. Cole
1974

Jessica Fayer
A spare, tidy novel

Beacon Hill dowagers, beware. Old Jessica Fayer has been mugged in Louisburg Square and lies sprawled on the cobblestones, her purse assaulted and its contents either ripped up or ripped off—pictures of saints, yellowing photos, charge cards and small bills.

This novel, like that pocketbook is spare and tidy, full of intricate confusion, a wealth of fine fragments, and small and not so small changes. It is like Jessica herself—chill, cutting, alarming, offbeat, haunting, strangely touching. Indeed, it is John L'Heureux's finest novel thus far.

Jessica was once Sister Judith, a 30-year-old nun who left the convent to marry a man whom she'd known only one month. Her new husband had once been in the seminary, but had fled when he found himself kissing another seminarian in an orchard. Now he owns a dismal rest home for crones. The marriage curdles. Having turned from God, Jessica turns to gin, then a black handyman, finally a middle-aged doctor. By then Jessica's 50, her husband's dead, and she's inherited the rest home and all the miseries of middle age. She can sell off only the former, and moves to Dartmouth street in Boston. Now a bit potty, she staggers through this last day of her life, pursuing ghosts from the past.

Myth has it that our entire lives pass in an instant before our eyes when we die, our best and worst moments in one dizzy compendium. A woman "trapped in the present tense," Jessica is dying and living it all over again. Simultaneously, she is 21 and brooding over a prayer book, or 30 and reaching for the gin, or 70 and lunching at the Top of the Hub, or dead. The Faulknerian presentness of everything heightens the abrupt transitions and flashbacks, while it steadies and contains her, propels her through a continuum of smoothness.

Most of Jessica's jostled memories are stark and forlorn. Especially impressive and spooky are the conversations between the old woman, Jessica, and Jessie Price, a lesbian philosophy professor who long ago, as an adolescent charge in the convent, had gone a little too gaga over Jessica (then Sister Judith) and loved her in sickening silence, unwisely and too well.

But all human loves end, Price sternly instructs her. What we mistake for love is simply our desire for being holy, which can only be attained from within. Human life surely ends.

Gunning toward Mrs. Fayer is a car in which unmentionable acts are being indulged in by the four young occupants. For all five it's the kiss of death.

But Mrs. Fayer's life, with all its sourness, is proof that human love is precisely the one thing that doesn't end. She silences the ghosts and turns her face toward the distant light. The headlights of that car. She is on a collision course all right—toward that mysterious wholeness, where reach no longer exceeds grasp.

—Lee Grove
1976

Desires
Short Stories Strung like Perfect Pearls

Anyone who writes knows a good short story is harder to deliver than a good novel. A novelist can hohum a while, waiting for inspiration; he or she can indulge in landscape description, or authorial introspection, or pages of nice-sounding dialogue that later turn out to be comparatively pointless. Most convenient, he can blather along for 400 pages or so, crossing fingers, hoping nobody will notice he never managed to come up with a plot.

But pity the short-story writer. He'd better come up with something on page one, or the reader drifts away. The smallest digression—a hangnail in a novel—is broken vertebra in a short story; it hampers all movement. And a short story without a plot is a wretched thing, a teen-ager without a tan shivering on the beach. Finally—shifting metaphors, the way you never can in a short story—like a Basque omelet, a short story rarely transcends its ingredients. No matter how competently it's put together it never gets to be *The Brothers Karamazov.* It's always a short story.

Resting Comfortably

But these are problems John L'Heureux doesn't have to worry about. Or perhaps he has worried about them, solved them, and now is resting comfortably somewhere with his feet up. Each story in this collection is pretty near perfect. And if that weren't enough, L'Heureux has solved the problem of short-story collections, the sigh of having to start anew every 20 pages, by placing each short work as carefully as perfect pearls strung by hand.

Desires contains stories in three parts: Marriages, Mysteries and—Desires. The "natural order" is reversed here; most people would suppose that desire comes first. But the first four stories set up a status quo and then point out that what we think of as the status quo is illusory, less a line of demarcation than almost anything we think we see in the real world.

The second section, "Mysteries," contains stories both bitter and farcical. They are bleak. Why is this man so depressed, and why does he have so much talent?

Desires addresses our own boredom and our shifting, mysterious daily life. We want to be loved, to possess, to be loved, to be possessed. We want to be at one with the Eternal, and if that does happen to us, we can't cavil at the terms.

If these short stories sound difficult, they are. Although many of them have appeared in popular magazines—Atlantic, Esquire, Harpers, the New Yorker—they are more than magazine stories; they are demanding, learned. L'Heureux directs the creative writing program at Stanford University, and evidently his stories go far beyond seeing daily life with a clear eye and not telling lies about it. Most of these stories bounce off another major work of art or are informed by a separate, distinctive, belief system.

Ricochet off 'Bliss'

"The Anatomy of Bliss," a story of misunderstandings, wretchedness, role-playing and final *rapprochement*, ricochets off Katherine Mansfield's simple classic, "Bliss." "The Priest's Wife" has as its subtitle "Thirteen Ways of Looking at a Blackbird" and you'd better know the poem. How else to appreciate the lines of dialogue, "It's snowing," and "It's going to snow," or even the story's 13 parts? And how to get the point of the story?

"Love and Death in Brighams" has the sonorous ring of other works, as do "Brief Lives in California" and "Answered Prayers." "The Consolations of Philosophy" works on its own as an exercise in the macabre and absurd, but the nightmares of terminal illness, mindless sex, and the hollow ring of used-up proverbs works even better if the reader has struggled through some Boethius, to see what he actually did have to say about the stern consolations.

Most of these stories are fables; that is, they are not anchored totally in what we think of as the "real world." Ordinary minds or less ambitious sensibilities might build these plots into something comfortable like science fiction or the standard fantasies of the day. But L'Heureux's other, invisible, world is the one some people think has been there all the time; a traditional Catholic world, the story of Christ crucified, of redemption through love, of a Devil whose face is indifference.

Two of L'Heureux's best stories follow these themes with hard elegance. In "Departures," a priest who has taken to the seminary as a convenient, social way to get away from people—seen as untidy, unattractive and downright nuts—commits the unforgivable sin, and never gets over it. His spiritual dryness finally takes his priestly powers away from him. And in "Witness," an independent Jewish woman who lives entirely in this world (she is a statistician and given to casual affairs) is afflicted, entirely against her will, with the stigmata.

The functions of American art, religion and philosophy are what L'Heureux is concerned about. Finally, *finally*, he seems to be saying, isn't our 20th-Century insistence on the perfectly realized, "realistic" external detail just essentially and eternally boring? Wouldn't it be better, for our art if not for our own individual lives, if we recognized other, larger grids on which to play out our dramas; wouldn't it make sense to postulate a supernatural good, an ecstatic Absolute, and then order our own lives as if these things existed? It would be more exciting that way, more "meaningful," more elegant.

These stories make no compromises. You either get them or you don't. Conversely, L'Heureux either succeeds at them or he doesn't. But their demands are refreshing. They are the opposite of a "good read." They are difficult, cranky, beautiful works of art.

—Carolyn See
1981

A Woman Run Mad
Nothing Recedes like Excess

If John L'Heureux had wanted an epigraph for his comic horror story, *A Woman Run Mad,* he could have used Goya's ambiguous inscription, in one of its possible translations: "The dream of reason brings forth monsters."

The book's four main characters represent in different ways the rational flower of our contemporary urbanity and the canker that eats it. They live in the gracious part of Boston, and they are more or less talented or charming or funny. The worst one is selfish and self-centered, but in a comfortably recognizable way. By the end of the book, they have fallen into madness and monstrosity.

In Sarah, a handsome and cultivated Brahmin, the madness is visible from the start, though misted by a vulnerable allure. Quinn, who taught English at Williams College and is now trying to write a novel, encounters her shoplifting a purse at the Back Bay branch of Bonwit Teller.

He is intrigued; and anyway, his writing is going badly. He follows her to her Beacon Hill apartment, only to be accosted on the doorstep by a young man who makes a crude sexual overture.

We learn at once—Quinn learns more slowly—that Angelo, the young man, is the brother-in-law of Sarah's brother Porter, and his lover as well. Uncontainably promiscuous, he spends his non-cruising hours reading Kierkegaard and Camus.

He has also been appointed to keep an eye on Sarah, who some years earlier had killed and mutilated a sexually sadistic lover and had escaped jail by a judgment of temporary insanity. When, at the end of the book, we learn the details of Sarah's mistreatment and her reprisal, they are so terrible as to blur the lines between the two and arouse a kind of desolate sympathy for her.

The above may begin to tell us what L'Heureux, a moralist of untrammeled imagination, is doing. But it takes us a long way from how he is doing it.

The horror in *A Woman Run Mad* is both serious and extreme. But we get to it gradually, by way of premonitions in which we have no real trust, in the course of a book that is blithe, witty and so coolly laid back as to constantly tell us that nothing really awful can be happening.

It is like dining in the most sophisticated of French restaurants, imagining we hear an occasional whisper of "poison" from the direction of the kitchen and reassuring ourselves that quite clearly we must have heard "poisson." And ending dead.

The blitheness begins with Quinn and his wife, Claire. She has prevailed over handicaps–orphanhood, poverty and a tendency to get fat–to become a brilliant Latinist and win a tenured position at Williams. Quinn, on the other hand, is shallow and self-absorbed. When he fails to receive tenure, he and Claire work out an arrangement under which he will spend the summer writing in a small Boston apartment and she will commute weekends.

There is an angry passion in Claire, but it is concealed—from herself among others—by a need to put aside her former ordeals and find gentleness and repose. She is actively winsome; she says "Quid?" for "What?", and when she succumbs to a cinnamon roll, she calls herself "Porcus ultimus." She clings to Quinn and is confident that he shares her commitment to marital coziness. For a while, we will get rather fed up with Claire.

Quinn does. Sarah's shoplifting seems exotic to him when he first spots her. So does the languorous and kinky sex she introduces him to when they finally get together. A touch of perversity is appropriate to the contemporary urbane. Even Angelo's cruising doesn't make him a monster, though it does get him savagely beaten up; he is genuinely kind to Sarah and loves to talk about ideas.

Quinn settles in to his summer fling. In his calculated way, he begins to write his novel about it. It is not long before Claire finds out what is going on; but she figures that she can wait things out. Quinn, on the other hand, begins to believe he would be better off ditching Claire and marrying Sarah, who longs to escape from her madness and her memories into a normal life.

Normality—as our time understands the word—and monstrosity are L'Heureux's poles, and he joins them with extraordinary dexterity. Sarah and Angelo, despite a sweetness that finally attaches us to them, are the monsters, seemingly. Quinn, despite his unlikableness, and Claire, despite her excessive striving, are the normal ones, seemingly.

The ending is not to be revealed, other than to say that it is bloody and grotesque and that normality and monstrosity become utterly indistinguishable. But it is in his style as much as in his plot that the author manages to connect his opposites. *A Woman Run Mad* is, for much of the time, witty and almost lighthearted. L'Heureux treats his characters somewhat in the manner of Iris Murdoch; even in their most matter-of-fact moments, we feel a horror closing in on them without knowing where it comes from. Conversely, representing large and terrible things, they are chatty and crotchety and sometimes very funny indeed.

There is the comedy of Quinn trying to turn his erotic sessions with Sarah into fiction. His notes read like a plumber's manual. "Wasn't writing about sex a lot like trying to re-create the first time anybody ate a baloney sandwich?" he asks himself.

L'Heureux, in a sentence, can convey enormous pain. Quinn has told Claire he will leave her. She walks out, swivels and tries to come back in; he holds the door shut against her. "They stood there, pressing wildly against one another, the heavy door between them," L'Heureux writes in a stunning reverse image.

The author is not always in full command of his odd and original novel. It bogs down in a series of internal monologues, particularly Claire's and Angelo's.

Having Claire discover a pistol in Angelo's bedside drawer early on, and introducing a peculiar little boy who spends his day sitting on the staircase and watching what is going on, may recall Chekhov's caution: Show us a pistol in the first act and we know it will go off in the last. Show us a watch bird at the start, we might add, and we know he will see something before the end.

A Woman Run Mad is quirky and unbalanced. Its excesses at the end hardly seem excessive, and that is the author's remarkable achievement. It is accomplished at the price of a large distancing.

It is hard to feel close to this talented book, which is clever most of the time and wise at least some of the time. It may be hard to love it. Perhaps it is not hard to dislike it. It is easy, in any case, to admire it and its author extravagantly.

—Richard Eder
1988

Comedians
God the Meddler

Plenty of writers these days dwell on man's inhumanity to man. John L'Heureux, not ignoring such every day cruelties, also is concerned with the inhumanity of God.

When the this former Jesuit's characters memorize a Bible story, they pick Abraham and Isaac. They muse that as soon as you let God into your life "he's got you." they question and get no answers; seek understanding and find cold comfort. Theirs is a demanding, inscrutable God; Job's God, not the Shepherd of the Psalms. Hating God is possible in Mr. L'Heureux's world; ignoring him is not.

God makes his presence known here a bit the way a horror or science fiction film let you know something strange is about to happen. There is a chilling lull—"It's quiet, Mike," the movie dialogue might go. "Yep, *too* quiet, Nate." Such films are crude. Mr. L'Heureux is agile, often very funny and invariably interesting.

Again and again the stories collected in *Comedians* (Viking, 209 pages, $17.95) update what Job learned: God's irony is absolute. Terrible things happen out of the blue. Good people are afflicted. Yet, several stories are touched by the miraculous—suggestions that peace and understanding can be found in the worst of moments. Death is something more than the quiet of the grave. God may be cruel, but he matters. In fact, he is inescapable.

In "The Terrible Mirror," the longest and best story in the collection, a woman tells her once-famous-and-smug, now foundering husband, that is she were to write a serious novel she would try to capture the random sprawl of life and "a single tiny thin *thin* thread of God's meddling in our lives." She says, "That's what would hold it together. That would be the only reality. The rest is madness anyhow."

Madness is another thread running through Mr. L'Heureux's work, a madness often tied to sex, as in his compelling last novel *A Woman Run Mad.* Sex breeds danger. Babies conceived are quickly stillborn. Passions conceived are quickly betrayed. People betrayed, most often women, take vengeance. Mr. L'Heureux's simplest stories are like fables. In the most obvious and least satisfying, "Nightfall," sex and the devil in the person of a motorcycle rider named Rory O'Toole (I said it wasn't subtle) trouble minds and disturb women's dreams in a quiet town.

It takes courage to live in Mr. L'Heureux's world: the courage to live with only small satisfactions and an appreciation of irony in place of hopeful prayers. Each must find his own courage like the priest, stripped of his belief, who comforts a dying man with his love in "The Expert on God." But even courage can break down. In "Rejoice and Be Glad," a woman who built a wall of her courage now can't stand the loneliness and would rip a hole in her wall for a moment of pity. Warmth and pity are in short supply. This is a cold world, in which the mind is more active than the heart. Triumphs are small, but not to be minimized. Faith and the daring to go forward are their own miracles.

Mr. L'Heureux's opening story, "The Comedian," can be read as a report on the trouble Jesus might have achieving a second coming by the means of his first appearance. A woman, her marriage and standard of living threatened by her impending baby, considers abortion. Doctors say the fetus is abnormally unrelated to its parents' chromosomes. But she can hear the baby singing to her so she goes ahead. Her baby comes forth in a dazzling blaze of light. It is a miraculous story.

Mr. L'Heureux is a manipulator of comedic and tragic masks. This is storytelling in which the wizard doesn't care that you know he is standing behind the screen, turning the wheel—just as, if you believe in miracles, you must believe that God has let us see his hand in their creation.

—Lee Lescaze
1990

An Honorable Profession
Alone in the Classroom

THERE IS any number of reasons to admire and respect the novels of John L'Heureux, among the most important of which are their firm roots in ordinary American reality. Though L'Heureux himself took refuge in an academic position at Stanford nearly two decades ago, he remains powerfully interested in the middle-class New England world in which he was born and raised, as well as that of the Catholic Church he served for several years as an ordained priest. His fiction has a grittiness that reflects this personal history, a quality found in the work of all too few of his fellow laborers in the writing-school groves.

It is characteristic of L'Heureux that the "honorable profession" to which the title of his 13th novel refers is high-school teaching: a most unfashionable subject by prevailing literary standards, yet one that is intimately connected to the country's daily life. That the high-school teacher could serve as window on that life seems to have occurred to scarcely any other writers of fiction, yet L'Heureux's instinct to use him as such is precisely right: Inasmuch as we now expect teachers to serve in loco parentis in every sense of the term save biological, it stands to reason that imagining our way into their lives could help us understand our own.

The teacher through whom L'Heureux attempts to do this is named Miles Bannon. He lives in Malburn, "a small New England town, a bedroom community for Boston and the computer industry along Route 128," and teaches English at Malburn High. He is 35 years old, a bachelor who as the novel opens is living with his mother; she is suffering from Lou Gehrig's disease, "trapped, alive, in a dead body." Like countless others caught in such circumstances, he is torn between "knowing someone you love is in excruciating pain [and] knowing that in the end the thing you feel most is the boredom," and as her condition deteriorates he suffers from the guilt of wishing for her death, as release for himself as well as for her.

When at last she does die he gains a measure of freedom, but he is haunted by a sense of responsibility for her death. This comes between him and Margaret Cleary, the young widow with whom he may or may not be in love, a decent but troubled woman who is herself torn between dependence upon him and uncertainty about her feelings for him. At first his emotional disarray leads him in an unlikely direction—a one-night stand with a suave homosexual—but soon it takes him into the bed of Diane Waring, the sexy and predatory young chairman of his department.

All of which adds up to a formula for trouble, but that's only the private side of Bannon's life. As a teacher "he was popular, he was smart, he was funny," but he has the bad luck to witness a painful incident in which a shy, unconfident boy is sexually abused by bigger boys in a game called Violation; this sets off a long but scarcely improbable chain of events in which Bannon's private and public lives become so entangled as to seem inseparable. In the end he is the victim of wild rumors and the object of unsupportable accusations, and his powers of survival are tested.

As this summary of the novel's plot suggests, An Honorable Profession threatens at moments to become a catalogue of such social ills as are routinely featured on the television programs of Oprah Winfrey, Geraldo Rivera et al.: child and spouse abuse, sexual identity crises, drugs and alcohol, geriatric decline, drunk driving—it's all there and a good bit more, and at times it comes dangerously close to excess. But what saves the novel from this is L'Heureux's lack of sentimentality, his refusal to lapse into easy, feel-good solutions. Here, for example, he describes the students' response to the death of a contemporary:

"In the corridors, girls were leaning against the lockers, sitting on the floor, hugging one another. They were sobbing, in an orgy of grief. It was luxurious. They loved it. Miles had seen this performance before and it was always the same. The girls sobbed and the boys moved silently up and down the hall, sulking, as if they were personally responsible for the death or as if they were offended that somebody else was getting all that attention just for being dead."

That's a smart and knowing observation, but L'Heureux doesn't stop at dismissing it as "a carnival of mourning"; he also understands that the kids "wanted to be deeply feeling, deeply caring people"—especially in an age that so highly prizes touchy-feely exhibitionism—and that "most of them were terrified at feeling nothing at all." Though it should be added that they are also terrified at the thought of their own deaths, it remains that this is a perceptive reading of the adolescent mind and of adolescent group behavior; there's a lot of this in An Honorable Profession, and it is among the novel's most rewarding qualities.

So too is L'Heureux's depiction of the teaching life. His portrait of the alliances and divisions within the teachers' room is vivid, in particular of those stirred up by a disagreeable young man who is trying to use his experiences at Malburn High as raw material for the great American novel. L'Heureux knows the teachers' world well—he was a high-school teacher himself for a while—and knows the tough lot they've been handed:

"How on earth was anybody supposed to teach composition? Even after all these years, [Miles] hadn't figured it out. You were dealing with a largely illiterate generation. They didn't read books. They didn't even read newspapers. They had no model for excellence other than television, where even Tom Brokaw said 'between you and I.' And Tom Brokaw was the high point of television literacy. You couldn't count MacNeil/Lehrer because students regarded MacNeil/Lehrer as a kind of punishment. It was hopeless really. It was poor old Sisyphus all over again."

But the teachers keep on keeping on, just as Miles Bannon struggles on against the various forces mustered against him. An Honorable Profession is a novel about survival both personal and professional, not merely that but survival with dignity and self-respect. It is itself an honorable novel.

—Jonathan Yardley
1991

The Shrine at Altamira
Sanctified Madness

As the prologue of John L'Heureux's *The Shrine at Altamira* warns, "We hear stories like this on television but we do not look, and when they turn up in newspapers, we glance away, because we know there are crazy people and people who are mad with love, but we refuse to know any more than that." Fortunately, L'Heureux has never been a writer to turn away from stories others fear. Perhaps his most ambitious novel, *The Shrine at Altamira,* is also his most successful; his sixth in a career that has examined the hardest questions of faith and love, it is certainly the most affecting.

When Maria Alvarez sees Russell Whitaker at a school dance, she wants him as much as she wants to escape her life in the barrio. Maria will not be satisfied by Russell's words of love, by his name or even his seed, but only by evidence that he wants her more than she wants him; she needs to see she has driven him crazy with love. At the end of this tragic and astonishingly redemptive novel, she will have been given more proof than she can bear.

As soon as Maria has snared Russell, she begins to tease him: She tells him she doesn't love him, cannot marry him. The effect of this torment is more profound than she guesses; once an abused child, Russell suffers her cruelties acutely, and unwittingly the girl has set the tinder for a conflagration that will destroy all she cares for.

Maria marries Russell, takes his Anglo surname and bears him a son, and then divorces him. After a period of alcoholic drifting, Russell returns to insist on his right to visit their son, John, but it is Maria who draws him. Spying on his ex-wife the night before he comes to pick up John for an overnight trip, Russell catches Maria in the arms of another man. Father and son never reach their amusement-park destination, because Russell drugs John and sets him on fire in a motel room; thus does Maria receive what she desired: proof that she has driven Russell mad with love.

John survives to endure a grueling series of reconstructive operations on his face. His surgeon is Dr. Clark, a man whose work is a vocation in the religious sense of the word, "saving what could be saved, repairing what could be repaired." Unable to reconcile himself to blatant evidence of evil, Clark confronts Russell in prison; he wants to discover that the boy's father is a monster, because if he is not "God's terrible mistake . . . What hope was there for any of us?" But the man Clark sees is merely human, someone who has sinned grievously and wants only to be punished.

After the fire, John replaces Maria in Russell's obsessive longing, and father and son are destined for a resolution that cannot include any other character. The boy dreams of union with his father; when he meets him for the first time after Russell is paroled, John realizes that the man who burned him is the only person who can look at his gruesomely disfigured face without flinching.

In his deepening crisis of faith, Clark seeks advice from an old priest who tells him that "What makes life so horrible is that even our salvation never comes in the form we would have chosen." So it will be with Russell and John: Their salvation, shocking and inevitable, cannot comfort Maria or anyone who witnesses the final consummation of their mutual passion. Around the central drama of sinner and sinned against, L'Heureux, in brilliantly economical strokes, sketches the range of human faith, from Maria's mother, whose belief accepts all, to Clark's psychiatrist, who says God is no more than an invention of the weak-hearted.

Ultimately, only the old priest can explain a story such as this: "God sanctifies us–he makes us saints–in his own way. Not in our way. It never looks like sanctity to us. It looks like madness, or failure, or even sin." John and Russell are so sanctified, and readers of this luminous novel will marvel that John L'Heureux has somehow conspired to redeem the unforgivable.

—Kathryn Harrison
1992

The Handmaid of Desire
Textual Politics

John L'Heureux's seventh novel is being promoted by its publisher as an academic satire. This is a bit like calling Moby-Dick a whaling yarn: true, but somewhat less than the full truth. The Handmaid of Desire concerns the English department of an unnamed university in California. The faculty is divided into two camps: fools and Turks. The fools are the older teachers, who actually enjoy literature. The Turks (excuse me, but isn't this tag a bit, er, "insensitive"?) are the younger set, who refer to literature as "discursive practices" and to whom all texts – "Flaubert's Bovary or . . . the label on a Campbell's soup can" – are of equal interest. Leader of the Turks is Professor Zachary Kurtz, a literary descendant of the ineffable Morris Zapp in David Lodge's Changing Places. Kurtz is plotting to enthrone himself as chairman of a renamed "Department of Theory and Discourse." He has invited noted theorist Olga Kominska to the university for an academic quarter, planning to make her his tool. Front man for Kurtz's coup will be Robbie Richter, a fool by age and inclination whose efforts to absorb literary theory are driving him to a nervous breakdown.

Kurtz and his colleagues are all prisoners of desire. Kurtz himself wants power, of course. Maddy Barker, who is a lesbian, suffers from "secret heterosexual urges for which she hated herself." Kurtz's wife wants to be rich. Fat fool Tortorisi wants tenure. Several of the faculty hanker for parenthood. Many of these desires are, of course, politically incorrect. All this is sufficiently clever and funny, and the reader who goes to this book looking for a send-up of campus politics will be well rewarded. However, there is more going on here than satire.

Whatever Kurtz's plans for Olga are, she herself has other ideas. Her ideas, in fact, are what the book is mainly about. There are hints that Olga is writing a campus novel, using these new colleagues of hers as dramatis personae. Of this one we read that she will "fit him in," of that one that she has "crossed him out." She seems to be able to manipulate them, to divine their innermost fears and desires and to give them what they think they want – hence the book's title. Kurtz's wife does indeed get rich, Maddy has sex with the campus stud, and so on. Even Kurtz's grand scheme achieves a kind of fruition, though with a very L'Heureuxian twist.

These self-referential murmurings become even harder to ignore when Olga takes Tortorisi under her wing and shows him how to get tenure: He must intimidate the deans by writing a satirical novel about the faculty! By this point one is not very surprised to catch sight of the author himself. Contemplating her own work in progress, Olga foresees that "at its heart there must stand an act of utter evil and absurdity . . . It must proceed from love gone wrong . . . " Which rather nicely adumbrates the last four novels of John L'Heureux.

So what is going on here? Or, as Kurtz asks of Olga: "Who ARE you? WHAT are you?" Is this some elaborate spoof of literary theory? Is L'Heureux deliberately blurring the accustomed boundaries between author, reader and text? Or what?

Well, possibly. So far as literary theory is concerned, this reviewer is George the First: I know nothing, and I desire to know nothing. Never having been seized by the urge to "deconstruct" any "text," I am, as it were, epistemologically challenged. I read novels for the old-fashioned reasons: to amuse myself and to satisfy my craving for an affirmation of moral order. So perhaps I have missed L'Heureux's main point, but I do not think so.

Olga is, in fact, a supernatural agent, with odd powers of clairvoyance into the lives of those around her. They are her creatures – though possessed of free will, liable to surprise her and capable of evil.

Yet Olga herself, though creator, is also of course a creation, who, at the very end, with a shrug of indifference to that foreseen act of evil, dwindles away like the Cheshire Cat "until she was no more than a mote in the eye of the last beholder." Here, in the book's penultimate paragraph, we glimpse at last the thematic thread that runs through all the author's fiction. "Beholder" or "believer"? L'Heureux was 17 years a Jesuit. His first novel dealt with a young Jesuit who endures a crisis of faith, and all his work since then has been a lament for the lost assurances of theodicy.

Thus, if I have got it right, *The Handmaid of Desire* is a satire wrapped around an allegory, a subtle literary joke that reflects the unique intelligence of a deeply thoughtful, intensely serious man.

—John Derbyshire
1996

Having Everything
A Human Exploration

Philip Tate, successful psychiatrist, looks into his wife's eyes and sees the emptiness left by pills and alcohol: "They had everything, their kids and their lives and their health, and they were good-looking, with enough money, and they loved one another - didn't they? - and yet they were wrecking it, somehow, in spite of themselves." Perhaps the ruin is not in spite of themselves but, rather, because of themselves, because of some deep and unacknowledged part of themselves. Take Philip's teenage compulsion to break into neighbors' houses. He has suppressed the urge, even the memory, for 30 years. Now, no less powerfully than his wife's desire for self-sedation, his urge is back.

John L'Heureux is perhaps today's most frightening novelist because his characters, for all their strange behavior, are not freaks or misfits. They are the people we see and know. They can be alarmingly close to being us. They are, as the title "Having Everything" suggests, people who will one way or another enact everything that lies within, including parts of themselves that are no less real for having been relegated to the shadows. Everything finds its expression, one way or another.

When Philip finds himself caught up again in his old house-breaking routine, for example, he knows very well that he is doing something very wrong and very reckless. He has just been appointed to a prestigious endowed chair at his university, after all; he is a man whose entire career is based on successfully analyzing human behavior. Even as he lets himself into a colleague's darkened house he can't quite believe he's doing it, but in a horrifying way this act is quite as much a part of him as are his many achievements.

"He should go home now, right now. He should get back into bed and thank the gods he had escaped from a crazy pointless act that could change his life forever. It was madness. It was lunacy." And yet he proceeds, and in the course of this gripping novel he discovers that his transgression has results entirely apart from whether he gets caught.

In that house he discovers the shadow-life of a couple he would have guessed had no inner life at all. Although the details emerge slowly, he finds himself caught up in the complicated dance of others' secret urges. His own wife, Maggie, descends more and more rapidly into her own abyss, and he can't help wondering if his compulsions have contributed to hers. As in many of L'Heureux's novels, the surface conduct is far less than half the story, as characters interact in ways and on levels that they do not fully comprehend, all their academic training notwithstanding.

Among the many wrenching ironies of *Having Everything* is that the most vile character is also the most perceptive. Hal Kizer, another psychiatrist, is into extremely dangerous sex, and he berates his wife for refusing to participate in his "seminars," as he calls them. He abuses her emotionally and perhaps physically, yet he seems entirely incapable of any shame or compunction. He even invites Philip to participate: "Relax, relax," Hal says. "I don't mean with me. I mean you could come along with me on one of my little seminars, just give it a whirl." Philip refuses. And yet he keeps his own compulsion more hidden than Hal does his, and Hal seems to sense as much. He tells Philip, "You and I are not that different, you know. Our problems, I mean, and our solutions to them. We're both at that moment in our lives when things can go anywhere."

After his conversation with Hal, Philip washes his hands, a classic subconscious gesture that even this trained psychiatrist cannot forego. He tells himself that Hal is "a totally dispensable human being." But if Hal is right about their similarity, then the thought ricochets back into Philip's own heart.

There can be no doubt that Hal was right about one thing: Philip's life can indeed go anywhere. The question for Philip is whether his better self will direct it. Here is where L'Heureux's novels, and especially *Having Everything*, become affirming, and all the more believably so for having reached their affirmation through an exploration of the most negative parts of human character. Confronting the worst in ourselves does not have to mean succumbing to it—it may, in fact, be our only hope of triumphing over it. In middle age, years after completing his professional training, Philip Tate has begun his true education.

To have everything, L'Heureux suggests, we must first lose the illusion of our own perfectibility. In doing so, we may lose so much more, for our lives can indeed go anywhere, but our only hope lies in taking the risk. *Having Everything* is an unforgettable exploration of what it takes to become fully human.

—Richard Wakefield
1999

The Miracle
Wonders Never Cease

MOST of the principal characters in John L'Heureux's admirable new novel, *The Miracle,* work for an institution, the Roman Catholic Archdiocese of Boston, that has been much in the headlines of late. L'Heureux's story is set not amid today's scandals, however, but in the early 1970's, and the offenses committed at St. Matthew's Church in South Boston by his protagonist, Paul LeBlanc—a lively, attractive priest in his early 30's—are not sexual but intellectual. LeBlanc preaches the primacy of individual conscience, he strenuously opposes the Vietnam War, and he's just a shade too glib when teaching high school students about papal infallibility. Moreover, like Maria in "The Sound of Music," he's always singing. His congregation adores him: "He is smart, energetic, filled with life. . . . You can tell him anything in confession because he is very broad-minded about sex and birth control. . . . He is what the modern church ought to be. They think."

But the men at diocesan headquarters—also known as the Kremlin—think otherwise. How do you solve a problem like LeBlanc? Their answer: a transfer to Our Lady of Victories, a church in a New Hampshire coastal town where LeBlanc (a la Bing Crosby in "Going My Way") is to care for, and take over the duties of, an ailing older priest, Tom Moriarty.

Two years pass. Then one day the rectory housekeeper, Rose Perez, goes home to find her 16-year-old daughter, Mandy, lying face down in bed, immobile and "deathly white." Rose summons a doctor, her landlord and LeBlanc. All of them examine Mandy; all are certain that she's dead. But Rose won't have it. Ordering everyone out, she prays fiercely to the Virgin Mary, demanding that her child be returned to life. When she lets LeBlanc back into the room, the girl is sitting up in bed, complaining of a headache. "It's a miracle," the priest whispers to Rose.

And then? It's easy to imagine where some novelists would take the story from here: word gets out about the miracle; the town is overrun not only with reporters (allowing the author to mount a facile critique of contemporary media culture) but also with the pious, the crazy, the desperate (in other words, a cross section of the spiritually parched modern world); the Vatican sends skeptical investigators whose bureaucratic cynicism and sophistication form a neat ironic contrast with Rose's simple and ardent piety. And at the center of the action would stand LeBlanc, his convictions about the church, his ministry and life's ultimate meaning shaken to their roots.

L'Heureux doesn't take that path. Instead of alerting Rome or the newspapers, LeBlanc responds to the astonishing event by fixating on—and badgering—Rose, whom he now regards (in none too orthodox fashion) as magical. Rose, for her part, is spooked by what she has experienced and refuses to admit that anything miraculous has happened. The other witnesses simply get on with their lives.

Indeed, you might say that getting on with life is, in L'Heureux's view, the whole point. If for some writers the fascination of this narrative's pivotal event would lie in the supernatural angle—the apparent violation of the laws of nature—what engages L'Heureux's interest is the human element: namely, Rose's motherly love. After the incident, LeBlanc surprises himself in the pulpit by concluding a homily about Lazarus as follows: "On the last day we will be asked the only question that matters. . . . 'Whom have you loved back to life?'" The truth that he has stumbled upon—and that the author plainly wishes to underscore—is that human love can restore, renew, revive. If Rose is magical, it is simply because she is human, and because she loves.

To be sure, as L'Heureux reminds us on nearly every page, people are imperfect, lacking in willpower, infirm in their beliefs, their lives cluttered and unfocused, their character traits largely impervious to change. ("Why can't I be humble?" Moriarty asks. "Why can't pigs fly?") Yet love can work through them to effect wonders. The human soul is the seedbed of the miraculous; it is primarily through one another that we mortal millions encounter the divine.

All of which comes as a revelation to LeBlanc. Deep down, he secretly hates himself for his joie de vivre, his hunger for human contact, his eagerness to be liked by others. What matters, he is convinced, "is sacrifice. What matters is to obliterate the self." Moriarty disagrees, branding such views as "fascist spirituality." LeBlanc's Kremlin interrogator, Monsignor Glynn, puts it another way. His young colleague, he maintains, has shut out God. ("You don't let him in, do you. . . . Why not let him in?") In his soul, in short, LeBlanc is a blank. The novel's epigraph, from Deuteronomy, sums up L'Heureux's message as bluntly as possible: "Choose life."

And life is assuredly what L'Heureux gives us. Himself a former priest and the author of a memoir entitled *Picnic in Babylon: A Jesuit Priest's Journal*—not to mention several earlier novels, like *Tight White Collar* and *The Clang Birds,* about priests and nuns at odds with the church authorities—L'Heureux has created in *The Miracle* a set of characters who feel fiercely authentic, not least in their contradictions, their changes of heart, their oscillations between strength and weakness, certitude and perplexity, ardor and apathy.

Now and then, admittedly, this authenticity wavers a bit. At times, for example, Moriarty and Glynn—both of them good, wise, salt-of-the-earth clerics—brush up against old-movie stereotypes. (Moriarty, cantankerous as Barry Fitzgerald in "Going My Way," refuses to call his ailment Lou Gehrig's disease: "It's my own goddamn disease, not some baseball player's.") Similarly, Rose's failure, after Mandy's reawakening, to even think of securing professional help or institutional care for the plainly self-destructive girl—or, at the very least, to make more of an effort to keep her away from her drug-addict boyfriend—may strain some readers' credulity, even if others find this inconsistency thoroughly human. Nor, frankly, is it entirely credible when LeBlanc—who appears to know the entire score of "Gypsy"—turns out to be heterosexual.

For all its realistic texture, *The Miracle* is also shot through with touches of biblical symbolism. Mandy's resurrection, like the Last Supper, takes place in an upper room; the building's owner is named Sal, as in salvation. None of this, fortunately, is overstated. On the contrary, one of the accomplishments of L'Heureux's novel—which is written in swift-moving prose of unaffected simplicity—is that, despite its nakedly upbeat message, it comes off as neither pat nor preachy but, rather, as a delicately nuanced portrait of recognizably human individuals making what they can of life.

—Bruce Bawer
2002